WORKING KNOWLEDGE

For Rollin Richmond —
a celebration for
working off.

Doug Harper

7/91

WORKING KNOWLEDGE

Skill and Community in a Small Shop

Douglas Harper

The University of Chicago Press

Chicago and London

Douglas Harper, associate professor of sociology at State University College
at Potsdam, New York, is the author of *Good Company*, a much-acclaimed photographic
portrait and narrative about tramps on the rails, also published by the University
of Chicago Press.

96 95 94 93 92 91 90 89 88 87   54321

Library of Congress Cataloging in Publication Data
Harper, Douglas A.
  Working knowledge.
  Bibliography: p.
  Includes index.
  1. Work.   2. Community life.   3. Repairing trades—
New York (State)—Case studies.   I. Title.
HD4904.H335   1987   302.3′4   86-30708
ISBN 0-226-31688-2

Line drawings by Suzan Harper

For Suzan

Contents

Acknowledgments

This book, of course, couldn't have been written without Willie and his family. A "thank you" seems hardly enough for their teaching, friendship, and companionship, and for permission to write. My own family participated too, maybe more than they know. Molly kept up a steady stream of interest and was often with me at Willie's. She took the photograph of Willie and me playing guitars, her first published work! Colter also knows Willie's world as a happy respite. He appears as a very young boy in a photograph taken some years ago when he and Willie were looking for frogs while I was photographing Willie's bridge. Colter spent many hours reading and drawing in the corner of my study, and asking when in the world I would be done so we could go play baseball, look for mushrooms, or whatever. It was a happy distraction and a warm memory. In many acknowledgment sections there is a perfunctory "thank you" to the author's spouse. My gratitude to my wife Suzan is genuine and abiding. She allowed me time—not easy given her enormously time-consuming greenhouse operation, which could benefit from a lot more help. She kept me on track with her wry questions. She knows the North Country better than I do, and she understands Willie because she shares his practical world. Her insight into what I have written has led me to constant rethinking. Finally, her drawings are what several photographic sequences needed, and it is good to have concrete evidence of her collaboration on these pages.

My mother and father helped with encouragement and at least two readings of the manuscript, during which my father poured out a great deal of copyediting ink. It is quite wonderful to feel your parents' support for your work, even as I get old enough so I ought, I suppose, to feel embarrassed by its importance.

Like all books this one has personal roots. I cannot think of Willie's world without remembering my next-door neighbor (when I was a teenager) and friend of many years, an elderly man named Red Breneman. Red was a fine tinkerer, and he taught me to appreciate quality in the repairs he performed on the vast array of machines that passed through his garage. Another personal source for this work is the teenage summer vacations spent working for my friend Elmer Frestedt at the Dry Dock Marine in my hometown in Minnesota. Until I met Willie I hadn't known anyone more adept than Elmer at finding his way through the intellectual and practical maze of mechanical repair. Elmer's and Willie's shops have different roles in their communities, but they are joined at the level of method.

In graduate school at Brandeis University, Professor Egon Bittner's careful explication of Weber's concept of rationalization quietly urged me toward this work. His article "Technique and the Conduct of Life," published some years later, fueled my simmering project. My two most important mentors, Jim Spradley and

Everett Hughes, both passed away while I was working on this project. It is my hope—a cherished hope I would say at the risk of sounding sentimental—that what I have written would meet with their approval. In the meantime Howard Becker has filled the role of mentor with detailed readings and discussions of selections, chapters, and finally a few versions of the whole manuscript. He has nudged me back on track in a way many of his students will recognize. My debt to Howie is deep.

Acknowledgment sections seldom mention the "unmet mentors" whose books and articles have played a particularly important role in the development of new work. Certainly one studies bibliographies to account for the flavor of new work. But there is usually a small group of authors who have been pivotal. For me those include Henry Glassie, John Berger and Jean Mohr, Robert Pirsig, and David Sudnow.

Several colleagues and friends put a great deal of energy into reading, advising, and editing. Greg Schaffner, Jonathan Imber, and George Psathas read the manuscript, in some cases several times, and offered in-depth comment, criticism, and encouragement. Toni Johnson read an early version and provided typically stern council. Tim Curry, Leonard Henny, Wayne Wheeler, Ricabeth Steiger, and several other colleagues from the International Visual Sociology Association gave insightful comments on the photographic dimension of the book. Walter Weitzmann helped me clarify the issue of reciprocity and reputation. Jane Edwards did the same for occupational folklore, and Debra Baiano read and criticized numerous drafts of the Introduction. Wayne Froman planted the germ from which many of these ideas grew in a Potsdam College lecture on technology and consciousness.

Unfortunately my publisher's policies forbid my acknowledging the contributions of individuals at the Press who did far more than their occupational role would demand to make this book happen in a way that is satisfying to us all.

Introduction

I moved to northern New York a number of years ago to teach in a small college. My department chairman noted my eight-year-old Saab station wagon and said, "Well, you'll be meeting Willie." It was an odd experience, repeated a number of times over my first few weeks in the North Country. One look at my old car and a new acquaintance would confirm that yes, I'd be meeting Willie.

It was soon necessary. No phone was listed, so on a Saturday morning a few weeks later I wove my way through fifteen miles of back roads and arrived at Willie's unannounced. I parked by a Saab a few years older than mine and walked over to a trailer surrounded by odds and ends of machinery. I knocked hard; a voice barked back: "Come in!" A man I took to be Willie sat by the window in the front of the trailer drinking coffee, looking grizzled and a bit formidable. He asked my business; I replied that I needed a windshield for my Saab, which I intended to sell. He looked out at my car, and I realized I'd been watched as I approached. After at least a minute of silence he said yes, someone *owed* him a windshield that would fit. He'd be picking it up one of these days, maybe in a week or two. When? How much? I thought to myself. But I kept quiet, feeling I was being sized up. Finally he asked me why I was selling the station wagon. I told him I had just bought an old Saab Sonnet, a discontinued and peculiar sports car. Only a few had been made, and from my first impression I didn't expect him to know anything about what was an esoteric and rather frivolous car. He replied that he had number 244 stored in a barn near Potsdam, waiting to be rebuilt. Its fiberglass hood, which amounted to the entire body of the car from the windshield forward, had been cut into seven pieces by garbagemen in Boston, who had found it sitting on a couple of garbage cans and decided it had been thrown away. The owner returned from a tool-buying errand to find them standing over his demolished hood with axes, ready to feed the pieces to the crusher. I nodded. I knew that scene, I said—I'd just moved to the North Country from Boston.

So began a working relationship. I ended up buying a house close to Willie's, and I've sought his help on construction, demolition, rebuilding, and the maintenance of a hundred-year-old farmhouse and an assortment of outbuildings. My old Saab has been followed by several slightly newer, most bought cheaply and rebuilt at Willie's shop. In the way of rural life, the shared work has led to friendship and to inclusion in community. Now, ten years later, I write about the man's work and how that work fits into the "web of group life."

Although much of what I will say about Willie points to his uniqueness, I know that in similar environments there are many like him. I am speaking of the rural North—areas like northern Maine, New England beyond easy reach of Boston,

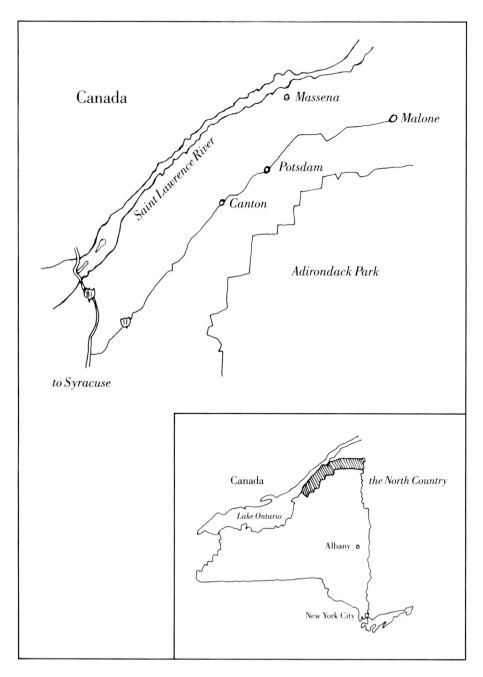

1 New York's North Country.

New York past the Adirondacks, upper Michigan, Wisconsin, or Minnesota, certainly the mountain regions of the West. These are poor areas, and outside the towns their populations are in decline. They are places of long, hard winters and great isolation. Agriculture, if it exists at all, is generally marginal. In the North Country the fields were first cleared from forests, and every spring they heave up a harvest of rocks that must be picked before the work can begin. The season begins late and ends early—farming reduces to a fight with mud and freezing, freezing and mud. Perhaps more natural uses of the land are the old forms of work that persist with improvised and roughly crafted technologies—cedar-oil manufacture, pulp logging, or maple-sugar making.

Mass culture has touched these areas relatively little. There are usually only one or two television stations with poor reception, no cable television outside the towns, and little choice among products, forms of entertainment, and jobs. Small businesses are less regulated than in more prosperous and populated areas, and zoning laws are only now beginning to be written and are loosely enforced. There is a feeling that you do what you must to stay afloat, and people work out among themselves the limits of those activities. John Berger wrote of people in a similar environment in northern England: "They form neither a proletariat nor a traditional rural community. They belong to the Forest and in the surrounding districts they are invariably known as 'the foresters.' They are suspicious, independent, tough, poorly educated, low church. They have something of the character once associated with wandering traders like tinkers" (1967, 89). At the same time, "[they] are not subject to the same frantic pressures as millions keeping up appearances in the suburbs. Families are less fragmented: appetites less insatiable: the standard of living of the foresters is lower but they have a greater sense of continuity" (1967, 133).

Although he was describing northern England, Berger could have been writing about New York's North Country. Saint Lawrence County, which forms its major area, is the largest county in New York State (at 2,768 square miles, it is nearly twice as large as the second-largest); and yet of the sixty-two counties in the state there are only three, all in the heart of the Adirondack Mountains, that have fewer people per square mile.[1] There has been economic vitality in the small Seaway city of Massena, but at present it is in steep decline because General Motors and Alcoa, the two main employers, have sharply reduced their operations. In general the rural economy of the region is depressed. This is even more striking given the economic contributions made by four colleges and universities situated in two North Country towns, Potsdam and Canton.

Geographically the North Country consists of a band of relatively flat to slightly hilly and rocky land bordering Lake Champlain on the east. The region extends along the Saint Lawrence Seaway about a hundred and fifty miles to the Thousand Islands, where the Saint Lawrence River flows out of Lake Ontario, bordering the Seaway on the north and merging gradually into the northern ranges of the Adirondacks to the south. The geography is important because in winter the mountains form a largely impregnable barrier and the only highway leading out of the region, Route 81, passes through a "snow belt" at the eastern tip of Lake Ontario that typically has the highest snow accumulation of any comparable area in the United States. The snow belt makes leaving the area in winter highly uncertain because of the infamous "whiteouts" that blow up in an instant, obliterating visibility on the freeway. The nearest major airport is 150 miles to the south in Syracuse, across the snow belt. In the North Country the leaves begin turning color in the last week of August and are gone by early October. The winter is as fierce as those of mid-Minnesota or northern Maine. All these factors isolate the area more thoroughly than any region I have visited in the United States. It is not uncommon to meet people from the North Country who have never been outside it, even for a visit.

Agriculture in the North Country is in decline and concentrated on fewer and fewer farms. It is still possible for single-family dairy farms to survive financially, but several economic, geographic, and social factors make it increasingly difficult.[2] Along the road I drive daily to work, for example, roughly half the farms have gone out of business during the past ten years. There are several abandoned houses and deserted, half-collapsed barns.

The isolation and the absence of what has become suburban American culture is the basis of life for people like Willie. Simply put, Willie's combination of mechanical and engineering skill makes him indispensable to others who depend on machinery, dwellings, and vehicles that are old and often improvised from leftover parts. Just as the region is "nonstandard," Willie is an iconoclast and individualist, a mix of traditional and modern knowledge and skills. Stating it this way, however, creates an incomplete picture. One of the fundamental realities of the area, by any reasonable index, is poverty. The difficulties posed by geography and material limitations are not always, even for people with Willie's skills, the basis of creativity and growth.

Willie's individualism, born in skilled work, extends to the relations he establishes as a businessman. To an outsider the things that influence whether a particular job is done may seem irrational—lucrative jobs may get stalled while Willie does small repairs for neighbors or works on projects of his own. The shop, however, operates by a logic that, while not obvious at first glance, ensures that Willie remains in control of his time and his energy.

Within the general environment of the rural North, Willie's work world is many sided. Each kind of work is done through a different system of exchange.

The overriding purpose of the shop seems, from the car bodies that surround it, to be Saab repair. This may be surprising to those who think of the Saab automobile in its recent incarnation as an expensive and elegant artifact of middle-class suburban culture. Traditionally the car had been the opposite: inexpensive and long-lasting, pragmatic and ugly; suited for rough roads and cold weather. It is an example of a technology suited to a region. The major components last unusually long, and the car engenders an unusual loyalty among its owners. At the same time, the early Saabs were demanding and eccentric. It was necessary to mix oil in the gasoline; at full throttle the two-cycle engine sounded more like a chain saw than an automobile. Even the colors drew attention: pea-soup green, grape, the dullest battleship gray, a faint lavender called "silver mink." And because the cars last so long it becomes necessary to maintain all kinds of things that most car owners never even think about. Tinker work. You get drawn in again and again. Just one, two, three small repairs, you find yourself saying, and the car will be like new. An odd reversal sets in; the car gets a paint job because it seems to deserve it.

Willie's talents and store of used parts make it possible for Saabs in the area to carry on for ten, fifteen, even twenty years. He knows their secrets and celebrates their unorthodoxies as well as their engineering sense. His shop is surrounded by Saab bodies slowly giving up their parts, moving piece by piece toward a state of final uselessness.

Broadly speaking, Willie does each type of work for a certain clientele, and each is bought and sold in its own way. Most of the rural poor cannot afford even the old Saabs. Willie's Saab business flourishes as much as he lets it largely because there are four colleges within twenty miles of the shop, and college students and professors tend to gravitate to old Saabs. Many make the trip and have work done in a reasonably standard manner for relatively standard fees. But even these dealings are influenced by many things that may keep Willie from his work. Among those who come to have their Saabs fixed are those who are least understanding of the way the shop operates and lack the patience required to deal with someone who enters into contracts in independent ways. For three years there wasn't even a phone in the shop or the trailer; you had to drive out and hope to have the work done on the spot or relay messages via citizens band radios and neighbors. It could be frustrating business, especially when a job got stalled for one reason or another. But there are also, among these people, those who appreciate Willie's skill and understand the balancing act he performs daily as he parcels his work out among more people than he has time for.

Others in the North call on Willie's skills and energies for different types of work. Among these are the farmers. Willie lives close to the seasons and feels their imperatives. It is said that he cannot be made to work for a person but will work for the seasons—when a farmer's equipment breaks down Willie will be there to repair it in the field or rebuild it in the shop. For this work everything else is put aside. Many of the farms are small, undercapitalized, and financially precarious operations trying to hold on for the next season or the next year. For this group Willie welds, rebuilds, and refashions machinery that more prosperous farmers would give up on—and possibly have. And several of these richer farmers rely on Willie to cope with the inevitable breakdowns from pitting steel against dirt and rock.

Aside from farmers, local people depend on Willie for a range of services that are more difficult to categorize. Most (but certainly not all) have little money and depend on machines and dwellings that are in ill repair, improvised, and makeshift. Willie might be called to do a welding job on a furnace in the middle of the coldest night of the year. A well casing may have to be repaired four feet underground because it was improperly installed fifteen years before. Plumbing and electrical systems that were haphazardly put in malfunction in ways that defy "expert" solution, and fixing them requires a mind that is not locked into established ways of seeing or doing. Willie may design a building, repair a sawmill, or build a vehicle to get a woods operation back to work. Local cedar-oil stills, well-drillers' rigs, and auto-wrecking setups have all been nursed back to health with Willie's repairing, redesigning, and rebuilding.

The payment for these services is complicated. It may include cash, but the jobs are generally not figured on a straight hourly basis. Much more often payment is in the form of barter or in favors either done in the present or to be called on in the future. Although Willie spends a lot of his time in this work, he makes little money from it. He often seems to take on jobs for the challenge they present. Indeed, it seems sometimes that the payment is mostly in the opportunity they present for Willie to work through a tricky problem.

This is work done for neighbors. It is not enough to live within ten or fifteen miles; to be neighbor to Willie you have to behave in a way that is routine in the shop but sometimes mysterious to outsiders. A person becomes a neighbor by passing informal tests, but you generally don't know what the tests are or whether you have passed until the time comes to ask for help. You become a neighbor by paying back, but the payment is seldom in kind. It is not that Willie will call and ask for help in the woods or on a project that needs an extra hand, though if you happen to be there when help is needed you will be expected (if you have the time) to lend that hand. The issue rather is whether you take the time for the small deeds; whether you put yourself in Willie's shoes and sense when a small social or physical contribution is needed. But you don't know if you are a neighbor until that moment when you are really in need. An exorbitant offer of money or a promise to do better next time you have a chance to repay a favor will not bring Willie out into the cold night. When you ask for help the chips are cashed in. If you have paid your dues—if you are a *neighbor*—Willie will come, and he will stay until the problem is solved. For these jobs often no money is exchanged. The most important work, ironically, is not sold but given.

Relations with customers and neighbors, however, are not always smooth or consistent. Deals and understandings routinely are broken or misunderstood and sometimes reforged. To understand the meaning of work, then, is to see it as a currency of community, the basis of exchange. To accurately describe these dealings that sometimes go sour is a difficult part of my task, because the people I have written about are my neighbors as well.

Issues regarding the ethics of disclosure have a long history in sociological field work, particularly in community studies. Dramatic examples I have thought about in relation to my study include the case of Robert and Helen Lynd, who published two books, ten years apart, on Muncie, Indiana. In the preface of their second book they review the reception of the first:

When *Middletown* first appeared, many people were immediately proud of the fact that the city "had been written up in a book"; the Chamber of Commerce used on its literature, "Selected as the Ideal American City," and this phrase was widely used locally. Shortly after its publication, the book was placed in the cornerstone of the handsome new downtown Methodist Church, and this elicited from the editor of Middletown's Democratic weekly the gleeful jibe: "If any of you people had taken the trouble to read *Middletown* and had read what it says about your Methodist Church . . . that book would never have been placed in that cornerstone. I am looking forward to the day when you people will read it and rush to tear down your 'cathedral' in order to get that damned book out of the cornerstone. Just because it *is* a wonderful book that tells the truth." (1937, xii)

Arthur Vidich and Joseph Bensman fared much worse with the publication of their community study *Small Town in Mass Society*, primarily because they described an "invisible government" of four men who were easily identifiable, although their names had been changed. A social movement arose in the town against the book, though the evidence was that few people had actually read it. A local newspaper described the culmination of the protest:

The people of the village . . . waited quite a while to get even with Art Vidich who wrote a "Peyton Place" type book about their town recently. The featured float of the annual Fourth of July parade today followed an authentic copy of the jacket of the book. . . . Following the book cover came residents . . . riding masked in cars labeled with the fictitious names given them in the book. But the payoff was the final scene, a manure-spreader filled with very rich barnyard fertilizer, over which was bending an effigy of "The Author." (Vidich, Bensman, and Stein 1964, 342)

These are obviously dramatic examples of the community response to having been written about, and in both cases the authors left the areas when the books were finished. Presumably the research did not have a lasting effect on their relationship with their subjects. When you write about people you intend to continue living among, the issue becomes considerably less abstract. Howard Becker summarizes ethical issues in regard to the publication of field studies and concludes that while social scientists ought to be wary of any kind of censure, in the end the only guide to what should be published is one's own conscience (1964, 279–84). I think that Becker is correct, particularly in stressing that we ought to ask ourselves whether the publication of specific material that is potentially damaging or embarrassing is truly needed. Bennett Berger (1981) also approaches the problem in a way I found helpful, by discussing the gap between the perceived and the lived reality among rural communards from a perspective that is never cynical or snide. Indeed, Berger notes that it is a function of all social life to do the "ideological work" of adjusting to the gaps between the perceived or idealized and the lived.

In the case of this book the issue is subtle and difficult. In allowing me to study his work and world, Willie has also given me a profound responsibility to present my results in a way that makes sense to him. On the other hand, the book has got to make sense to the part of me that is a sociologist, and though we live in the same world geographically and share a friendship, my training certainly leads me to see things from a different perspective than that of most of my neighbors. . . . Sociologists are probably always strangers, in some sense, to the communities they live in. Throughout this book I have included stories about how specific individuals sometimes broke informal rules and temporarily changed their relationship with Willie. I have been in this position myself, particularly as I worked through "city" ways to learn how to behave in a rural environment where reputations are long-standing and small acts have enduring importance. The people I have written about are often my friends and neighbors, and though I have changed their names in this narration, they may be able to identify themselves. To eliminate this material would be to not tell the whole story, or at least the most complete account I can provide. My great hope, one I have thought about a great deal, is that the individuals whose stories I've told will accept the sociological purpose of the telling and not be personally offended.

I have organized my study of Willie's work into two general topics. The first section of the book is called The Nature of Work; the second, Contexts of Work. The categories that make up these distinctions have emerged through a dialectic process of ongoing observation and reconsideration—an example of what Glaser and Straus call "grounded theory."[3]

First I discuss Willie's work in terms of how it resembles that of the premodern *bricoleur* characterized by Claude Lévi-Strauss. To examine the work process more deeply I then discuss Willie's "deep knowledge" of materials; the corporeal or kinesthetic knowledge evident in the work; and the relationship between work and time that is found in the shop. The overriding definition of the nature of work is based on a discussion of the evolution of skill in modern work. The skill found in Willie's work is important to understand because, along with many other skills in modern life, it is disappearing. Willie's kind of skill is an element of an earlier cultural form continuing in a small pocket removed from the general culture.[4]

The second broad topic of the book concerns the relationship between Willie's work and its social, geographic, and economic contexts, including Willie's lived definitions of use value in contrast to general cultural values of planned obsolescence. This can be stated as the ecology of Willie's life—the way his work continually redefines the relation of people's material culture to their geographic and biological setting. Other contexts of work include how Willie defines himself through his work and how his work leads to a sense of acting and being in the community.

I have studied Willie's work from several angles, but the categories I have ended up with are my own.[5] In naming and classifying its elements, I have separated out aspects of Willie's taken-for-granted world, presented them back to him in discussions we have recorded, and finally used them to translate Willie's experienced world into terms that those unfamiliar with the culture can understand.

METHODS

Rather than exactly defining my methods, I will show with a brief "natural history"[6] how the study emerged and developed. This natural history is necessarily autobiographical in that the research has been a part of the past few years of my life and my family's.

As a beginning sociology professor I often taught field methods by having students take photographs of their subjects and their social environments. During my first five years at the SUNY college at Potsdam I revised my doctoral thesis several times to eventually publish a book (Harper 1982) that included photographs and a fieldwork narrative. I was thinking a great deal during these years about the possibility of a fresh research project that would integrate fieldwork and photography. The demands of my life—like, I suspect, those of many beginning professors with a heavy teaching load and a young family—made it difficult to begin fresh new work. My photography had ground to a halt, and the only thing I had written were several versions of my book. During these years, however, I spent a great deal of time with Willie. He was an adviser and problem solver on many difficulties we encountered with our machines and building projects. At the same time, I saw that the problems we faced living in a rural environment were similar to those of many in the neighborhood, and as I observed Willie I began to see how his work combined skills that were important to a wide range of people.

Eventually I was able to free enough time and energy to begin a fresh study. At first I was interested in a purely photographic study of Willie's shop. But even as I got to know Willie, I had a hard time getting down to serious photography, primarily because I didn't want to call attention to myself. At first I hung around in the background taking snapshots in an offhand manner. The photographs were uninteresting because the details of the work were missing. Furthermore, the shop was dark, and using a strobe would have drawn yet more attention. I realized after a few unsuccessful attempts to photograph this way that I would have to explain my plans—as, of course, I also needed to do for ethical reasons—and to begin photographing in a forthright and even aggressive manner.

I was able to approach the subject partly because of my first book. Willie saw the process of revision, reconsideration, and further revision as similar to his own working method. Seeing the finished book gave concrete form to our ideas about a second book. In part, I think, because Willie was interested in the subject matter of the first book, the railroad tramp, he accepted the idea that we would collaborate on a second. Like the tramps, he felt that only a few like-minded people understood his type of work and how it was part of a functioning rural neighborhood.

I began photographing with a strobe and a short telephoto macro lens to concentrate the camera on hands and materials; the small details of jobs in progress. Switching periodically to a wide angle lens made it possible to photograph the work in its context. The photographs, lighted by the strobe, showed the detail I had wanted from the beginning. As long as I took care not to flash the strobe in Willie's face while he was working it did not pose a serious problem, though it made my activity the center of attention in the shop. For a while some of the men came around less often, and I wondered if the photographing irritated them enough to keep them away. Willie said they came and went as they pleased and left it at that.

There was, of course, the question of what to photograph—a question more complex than it first appears. Although photographs adorn sociological textbooks, these are probably the worst places to look when considering how to use photographs in research. The relationship between text and images in these books is generally casual. The illustrations have usually been added by editors to "dress up" text, and the level of description in the photographs is almost always very low. The utter obviousness of the legends reinforces the image that sociology mostly restates what everybody already knows. Unfortunately most social scientists tend to think of photographs as unnecessary but sometimes pleasant (and sometimes distracting) additions to the real (written) work.

However, some sociological and anthropological studies have made good use of photography as social description.[7] And there are also documentary studies that sociologists would do well to imitate.[8] But the issue is complicated by the varying levels of quality within the documentary tradition. There may be a similar relationship between journalism and sociology and photojournalism and visual sociology, best summarized by the idea that while the primary purpose of journalism is communication, the purpose of sociology lies more in explanation. Yet these can easily become self-serving generalizations.

In less useful documentary studies the depth of the involvement, and thus the level of understanding between photographer and subject, may be slight. The result is best summed up in Becker's comments:

When social documentary photography is not analytically dense the reason may be that photographers use theories that are overly simple. They do not acquire a deep, differentiated and sophisticated knowledge of the people and activities they investigate. Conversely, when their work gives a satisfyingly complex understanding of a subject, it is because they have acquired a sufficiently elaborate theory to alert them to the visual manifestations of that complexity. In short, the way to change and improve photographic images lies less in technical considerations than in improving your comprehension of what you are photographing—your theory. (1974, 11)

The first photographs I took at the shop lacked any coherence from Willie's perspective. They were really photos by an interested outsider, seeing exotic forms in the routine of the shop. Howard Becker would say I lacked a theory, which in his terms is "a set of ideas with which you can make sense of a situation while you photograph it. The theory tells you when an image contains information of value, when it communicates something worth communicating. It furnishes the criteria by which worthwhile data and statements can be separated from those that contain nothing of value, that do not increase our knowledge of society" (1974, 12).

The question of what to photograph became, in fact, the question of how to see things at least roughly as Willie saw them. The goal of the research was to share Willie's perspective. It is a gradual and incomplete process, now ten years long and not over yet.

My efforts to gain a perspective close to Willie's, however, have been systematic. The primary method has been a process called "photo elicitation," first described by John Collier (1967) as a way to integrate photographs into interviews.[9] In the photo elicitation interview the subject and the interviewer discuss the researcher's photographs, giving the interview a concrete point of reference. This approach is different from other sociological interviews because a photograph, rather than an interviewer's question (which may or may not make sense to the individual being interviewed), is the focus of attention. Roles are reversed as the subject becomes the teacher. The photo elicitation interview also points the photographer in new directions as the subject tells what is missing in the photographs and what should be included in subsequent ones.

Organizing the photo elicitation interviews was difficult at first because explicit schedules at Willie's have a way of getting lost in the demands and moods of the immediate. It wasn't clear where we would work, since with two young daughters, his house is full of activity, while customers and friends drop in at all times of the day or evening. Once begun, however, the interviews went smoothly. Willie matter-of-factly discussed the techniques of work that show the depth and extent of his knowledge, details of exchanges of favor and material that make the analysis of the relationship of work and community clearer, and "biographies" of machines and even parts that show how Willie makes the leftovers of the world into replacement parts and even new machines.

I organized the interviews by selecting photographs around specific themes and projects. Having in mind a general theme for each of the sessions, which usually lasted two to four hours, I brought along several photographs that were related directly or indirectly to that theme. Many of the most useful photographs were sequences showing the progress of a job or project. The time represented by a sequence of photographs might represent as little as a half hour, in the case of a particular repair, or as long as seven or eight years. Photographs of a particular piece of machinery or a part or a completed project were also useful. The key was to get beyond the obvious. Willie could look at a series of images and sum up the repair into an astonishingly brief statement. It was then necessary for me to get him to elaborate by asking questions or offering my own observations. We fumbled along on some of the photo sequences that did not go anywhere, and other photographs that I would not have expected to yield a particularly telling insight provided just that. In the beginning interviews I had a tendency to fill up silences with statements that praised Willie as a master of esoteric technologies. As the interviews continued, I became more comfortable with the silences (which generally meant that Willie was studying the photograph and thinking, rather than waiting for verbal cues or support) and, as I learned more about the subjects of the photographs, gained more confidence in the questions I did ask.

We eventually completed over thirty hours of interviewing. I then transcribed the interviews, producing about three hundred pages of text. All the photographing, interviewing, and transcribing took place during summers, vacations, and weekends, so there were periods of up to five months between interviews, giving the project a gradually mounting momentum. As I transcribed an interview session I digested the material and integrated it with previous interviews, field notes, and photo sequences. The final writing included the juggling and continual rearrangement of small sections that were selected directly from the interviews, field notes, and analytic passages.

I also collected field notes in a traditional manner. During the three years when I gathered the bulk of the information, I wrote short narrative passages almost every time I returned from a visit to the shop. These are descriptions of time I spent with Willie, working, helping, or just visiting. The vignettes tell stories that include the give-and-take between Willie and his customers and friends; they may tell how a job comes to be done or not done. Willie often tells stories as he works, usually to make a point about something that has just happened or to take a break from work. Several of the fieldwork passages retell these stories.

These field notes were a journal of observations that guided me through early stages of writing. At the same time several of these vignettes (I eventually wrote over fifty of them) revealed insights I thought were particularly telling. Some work as short stories: presenting characters and developing a small conflict and its resolution. In telling the story of the shop, they often told the story of the neighborhood. As I began writing the manuscript I thought that though I might include excerpts from these vignettes, there would be no place for them to appear intact. I eventually reconsidered this decision when I saw an important voice being lost. The book now includes Willie's voice and mine, both moving from analysis to narrative. By keeping these voices intact I retain the nuances of meaning embodied in each. To organize the book I have worked partly like a film editor—juxtaposing images to text and laying on different levels of sound as I build from narrative to analysis. The physical structure of the book thus becomes an important element in itself.[10]

Although I can describe my different approaches and themes, I have found at times that the closer I look in the process of research, the more difficult it is to be sure of what I've learned and the harder it becomes to communicate that tentative understanding. It is the opposite of what common sense would suggest. Seeing something closely ought to make it easier to understand and describe. John Berger says that the fieldworker, eager to see everything possible, is "inevitably half-blind, like an owl in bright daylight." I am drawn to that description, for it communicates how I see my own limitations as a fieldworker and the limitations shared by all attempts to describe and analyze.

My work draws on a number of disciplines but does not fit precisely into any of them. As a community study its emphasis on the life of a single individual is unusual. The method of observation is common to anthropology, and a case study approach has a long, if controversial, tradition in sociology.[11] This is a study of material and folk culture, with an unusual emphasis on visual methods. I feel I have improvised a method of observation and reporting that is similar in some ways to the way Willie takes on a task. Still, it is hard to precisely categorize what I have produced. Rather than attempt such a categorization, I can get a certain sense of relief and perhaps inspiration from Henry Glassie's resolution of his own biographical/community study:

We have one enterprise. We could call it historical ethnography or local history or folk-lore in context or the sociology of the creative act or the ecology of consciousness—the potential for flashy neologism seems boundless—but whatever its name, study is distorted and reality is mangled when disciplines harden into ideology, categories freeze into facts, and the sweet, terrible wholeness of life is dismembered for burial.

. . . if work is good old categories will slip and shift, and then melt away as we find the place where social science joins the humanities, where art and culture and history, time and space, connect, where theoretical and empirical studies fuse. (1982, xiv)

The key, I think, is a simple idea that is the base of all ethnography. I want to explain the way Willie has explained to me. I hope to show a small social world that most people would not look at very closely. In the process I want to tell about some of the times between Willie and me, thinking that at the root of all sociology there are people making connections, many like ours.

2 Willie's shop, aerial view.

3 The exterior of Willie's shop.

Part I   THE NATURE OF WORK

The Evolution of Practical Labor

To understand Willie's work we must go all the way back to the Iron Age. Between Willie and the ancient worker, however, are several broad steps in the evolution of work. As large categories, these steps include the prestandardized, preindustrial handwork forms of production; the standardized, preindustrial forms (craft or artisan work); the industrial or factory form of production; and modern automated, computerized work systems. These stages correspond to large historical periods, but they overlap and sometimes coexist. The roots of Willie's work are in the prestandardized handwork forms of making that precede even the craft or artisan stage.

The first stage came into its own during the Iron Age, which began in Europe about 500 B.C. and gave birth to the medieval smith. For well over a thousand years in Europe, the smith was the principal metalworker. Advances in iron-smelting techniques (principally the development of the blast furnace in the fifteenth century)[1] eventually made early forms of large-scale production possible. The Iron Age was preceded by a Bronze (and Copper) Age in which sophisticated metallurgical practices were also well developed. The social use of metal and the social character of the smith changed fundamentally, however, as iron achieved dominance in society. The Copper and Bronze Age smith came from a caste that primarily produced artistic and religious objects for the ruling groups. The softness of copper and bronze, compared with tempered steel, made practical objects less useful than those that followed from the hearth of the ironworker. Finally, the alloys used by the pre–Iron Age smiths were rare and beautiful and were valuable for aesthetic as well as practical reasons.[2]

The beginnings of technical knowledge, and the origin of the "type" of which Willie is a modern version, came from the period of the handworking of iron. Objects made from iron and steel, unlike those of copper and bronze, were used in the daily life of the common people rather than by specialized groups such as soldiers or rulers. Although iron ore was generally much more abundant than the earlier metals, smelting iron is much more difficult and mysterious than smelting copper, silver, gold, or any of their alloys. Smelting iron requires a higher temperature, and though carbon is needed in the smelting process, it was not understood until the eighteenth century that it acted both as a reducing agent and as an alloy. The ironsmith cooked his ore with charcoal and pounded the molten mass to separate the slag from the metal in a long, arduous, and mysterious process. It was practical knowledge—intimately tied to the material and lacking scientific basis—that guided his hand. But the smith formed the implements, weapons, utensils, and tools that moved people into a premodern stage and maintained them there for at least a thousand years. We think of the blacksmith as a farrier, but it was not until the ninth century, hundreds of years after the smith had become a fixture in communities in Europe, that horses were shod.[3]

The smith at the rudimentary iron-smelting oven and the forge extended human effort in a significant way. Technology itself was worked into new forms with each object made. Fernand Braudel writes: "In a way, everything is technology; not only man's most strenuous endeavours but also his patient and monotonous efforts to make a mark on the external world; not only the rapid changes we are a little too ready to label revolutions . . . but also the slow improvements in processes and tools, and those innumerable actions which may have no immediate innovating significance but which are the fruit of accumulated knowledge: the sailor rigging his boat, the miner digging a gallery, the peasant behind the plough or the smith at the anvil" (1981, 334).

The knowledge embodied in this work forms a unity; whole processes are controlled by a single individual. Fixing and making are but different points along a continuum. The individual who possesses these skills performs tasks that are essential to the community and has a status equal to that importance. The community, in this case a small, intimately connected group of people living close to their natural environment, relied on the smith to make several of the necessities of life—the weapons people used to kill animals and protect themselves from their enemies, the utensils to cook soups and gruels in pots and meats on spits, and the tools used by the carpenter, the other great fashioner. The more isolated the community and the more hostile the environment, the more important was the smith's work. The Icelandic settlers in Greenland, for example, tolerated the man who smelted and forged the iron ore even though they thought he was the devil incarnate. It was through his work that they hunted the seal, the walrus, the polar bear, fought with the Eskimos, and repaired their ships and built their houses.[4] The smith of the Dark Ages in Europe was suspected of keeping dark secrets. Henry Glassie, for example, writes of Ireland: "In ancient days the smith was a magician, and in the days of the old people his mundane product was counterposed to otherworldly mystery."[5] The connection of the blacksmith to magic and sorcery also has to do with the awe common people felt at his ability to transform the very material of the earth, seemingly magically. George Ewart Evans adds: "The smith was a great figure of interest in his own right even before horses were his chief concern. Moreover, the fact that he was deified or highly honoured in so many cultures—Tubal-cain, Hephaestos, Vulcan, Wieland or Volundr—is a measure of the awe with which he was regarded in early times. At first, too, a man who could hammer sparks of fire out of an object was looked upon with fear, as someone who was in league with the Underworld or the Powers of Darkness"

(1966, 166). Metal objects were also made into religious artifacts, lending a sense of the sacred to the profane creations of the smith's hands. The smith in contemporary developing countries often has a similar status.[6]

Willie's working knowledge, and its role in the community, is like that of the ancient ironsmith. The unity of the knowledge is complete; the worker who forms the object either uses it himself or makes it for members of his immediate community. Repair is only an extension of making and routinely includes modification or transformations of the technology.

This prestandardized handworker gave way to the artisan or craftsman. The artisan did the same thing over and over, but he did it very well. The craftsman's labor was eventually organized into working groups where the oldest and the most accomplished—the masters—held the highest status. This evolved to the guild, through which workers were trained and certified as competent. The worker who made things for the community no longer gained his social identity directly through the community's judgment of his work. In this way the guild is an early form of the institute training of modern mechanics—a process in which the training as well as "certification" becomes formal and concrete, rather than informal and embedded in the social groups to which it is attached. Blacksmiths' work, as George Ewart Evans shows us, also became organized into a master apprentice arrangement, though from his description of the English smith of the nineteenth century we learn that the formal training system did not entirely remove the worker from the judgment of his community (Evans 1966).

By the fifteenth century the development of the blast furnace and water-powered bellows and hammers led to the production of metal goods in small "factories." The factory may have consisted only of a master and three or four other workers, but the products, from weapons to agricultural implements—long before the Industrial Revolution and the rise of machine production—were increasingly standardized and made for nonlocal markets. The immediate connection of the work to the needs of the community was broken, and the mentality of the earlier worker, who controlled the whole process of work, was fragmented as several people each did a small part of the larger construction over and over.

With the development of coke as a fuel, cast iron and then steel could be manufactured on a much larger scale. With these changes iron and its derivatives ceased, for the most part, to be the materials of independent individuals working to fulfill a community's needs. The exception, in the case of metalworking, was the blacksmith, who continued to shoe horses and sometimes repaired and fashioned farm implements and machines. The blacksmith can be understood as a figure who extended an earlier method and, we can infer, the consciousness of the primitive maker into an era where they were becoming extinct. The continued role of the smith in northern Europe was in large part due to (but not limited to) the growing importance of the horse. Speaking of the late Middle Ages, Braudel writes that "the shoeing smith was a person of substance, his establishment being rather like the present-day garage" (1981, 352). This tradition continued in the American colonies, roughly until the general adoption of the automobile and mechanized farm equipment.[7]

Although work in the crafts period became increasingly organized (regulated in Europe by guilds industrywide and by the shop master locally), and though the products became more standardized and were more and more intended for non-local markets, the old way with its mélange of hand and theoretical knowledge continued to be important. It did not disappear with the rise of craftsmanship; rather it coexisted, and in some artisan work it was the dominant approach. This is shown in Ronald Blythe's modern study of an English village. The wheelwright (who is also the blacksmith) speaks of his experience as a young worker:

My father was a wheelwright and my uncle was the blacksmith. I was the only apprentice and they were very strict. "You've got to have a good eye," they said. "Everything that's got to be done in wheelwrighting has got to be done by the eye. You've got to let your eye be your guide." They were right, of course. What we do here isn't like the ordinary carpenter's work. When you get the hub of a wheel it has to be morticed once and only once first go.

. . . Heaps of times I did a shaft and I'd think, "That's lovely!" Then my father would rub his hand up it and say, "Why, boy it ain't *half* done!" . . . There was no second chance in so much of what we did. It made us cautious but at the same time it made us willing to take a risk. It was as much in the eye as in the hand. There was a moment when you had to say *Now!* Then you could breathe again. (1969, 150–51)

Egon Bittner calls this kind of work "practical labor," which "is always controlled by full regard for the timely and local features of the environment within which it takes place. Accordingly, one would have to say that [practical labor] . . . involves the exercise of an intelligence that comes into its own in communication with the concrete and actual realities of its natural setting" (1983, 253). Bittner stresses that practical labor consisted of disparate methods, connected to specific material circumstances. By themselves these methods represent a stage of technological development that is quite limited. The Industrial Revolution depended upon organizing and systematizing these separate and unique techniques that came out of actual situations of life. This made a more advanced level of technical complexity possible, but it also changed the relation between knowledge and the individual worker. As Bittner writes, "technical effectiveness is no longer perceived in relation to concrete purposes, but in terms of an abstract, aimless idea of effectiveness." The work directed to achieving technical effectiveness is "no longer guided by a live intelligence, fallibly attuned to actual circumstances; instead it is determined by a detached and externalized intelligence embodied in a formula" (1983, 253).

The general transformation of technique in society is part of an ever-widening split between the envisioning of a thing (engineering) and its production. With each stage of production the complexity of knowledge increases while the role of a single individual in relation to the overall task of engineering and production decreases. The result has been, as explained in many familiar analyses, the alienation of the worker—his or her separation from a sense of purpose, separation from self as well as community.[8] This process of alienation can, from one perspective, be summed up as the separation of the worker from the *knowledge* that once guided the work.

The result of the ever-increasing division of labor, wrote Max Weber, is rationalization.[9] Rationalization describes the process through which social organization becomes more systematized as the division of labor becomes more elaborate. Rationalization makes the worker an ever-smaller cog in an ever-larger social organization. Although the organization of a rationalized society is more efficient, the human experience becomes ever more routinized. The knowledge embodied in the social organization increases as the working knowledge of individual participants decreases. The method of work becomes increasingly specific, easily knowable, and predictable. The mind called forth by a rationalized society also becomes more objective, which means that solutions to problems are more definable and predictable. While all work is touched by rationalization, certain kinds of work are more easily made routine than others. *Making*, for example, evolves to mass production, a fully rationalized system. Making the machines that guide and control the mass production (the work of the millwright), however, depends on the method and mind of the artisan, and thus it preserves that earlier method. *Fixing*, in a general sense, extends a yet earlier mind and method, that of the original fashioner.

Making and fixing are eventually guided by different kinds of knowledge, making being dominated by the limited knowledge of the machine tender and fixing by the knowledge of the earlier mind that stood in the same relation, as its inventor, to the technique. This, however, is a lag rather than a permanent separation. As making becomes increasingly rationalized there are, for a time, individuals with knowledge that allows them to see beyond the elements of a technique to its overall purpose and coherence. This knowledge is the "live intelligence, fallibly attuned to the actual circumstances" of life. It is the knowledge in which making and fixing are parts of a continuum.

In a rationalized society, however, fixing is increasingly dominated by the same processes, and calls forth the same knowledge, as does making. This is what I have called the "rationalization of repair," the extension of "deskilling"[10] to an area of work where one would expect to find old forms of method and consciousness. Because one of the largest arenas of fixing in modern society involves maintaining automobiles, and because much of Willie's method can be found in his work on automobiles, when I talk of repair, it is generally automotive repair to which I refer. The theoretical issues, however, extend to all forms of repair in society.

The rationalization of repair has several aspects. As repair becomes rationalized, it becomes more objective and less "intuitive." I use the word "intuitive," however, with concern that Willie's method not be thought of as essentially mysterious. Much of what he has to say in response to the photographs and to my questions demystifies what, to the uninitiated, seems like an intuitive method. Still, I think the interplay of specific and detailed knowledge that is called upon in a genuinely complex repair is objective in such a way (understandable to the actor, barely comprehensible to the observer) that to label it intuitive does lend, at least for now, the proper perspective.

Similarly, the method of rationalized repair is more inductive than deductive, depending on small steps without a guiding consciousness that understands the whole machine. The rationalized repair, as one might expect, deals more with specific components of a machine that are defective than with the overall integration, or tuning, of its components.

As automotive repair becomes more rationalized, repairmen are trained in schools and certified by earning degrees. This is a key distinction. This training replaces knowledge gained in life, probably from one's father, as a method of informal certification, in this case the acceptance of one's work by the community. With the professionalization of repair, customers assume a repairman's competence on the basis of his formal certification. The "screwdriver and wrench" mechanic, working out of a small shop, taking care of his or her neighbors' needs, is replaced by people in clean white smocks commanding a baffling array of repair machines. The attitude one brings to the modern shop is similar to one's attitude toward one's medical doctor. The customer does not have the knowledge to evaluate what is happening in the repair and is forced to assume that their training has equalized all the mechanics who work in a now generally large shop. Certainly one's trust is shifted from the individual repairman to his or her quasi-professional status.[11]

The formal training of the modern repairman emphasizes the objective character of repair—it treats the knowledge of repair as in the head (although, of course, the education generally includes "hands-on" experience) rather than in the hand or in both head and hand. Of course, many who attend these courses of study have had long years of "apprenticeship" at shops like Willie's, as sons or daughters of men like Willie, and in these cases the formal training is probably, for the most part, a systematizing of their existing knowledge. But as the small shop gives way to the large garage and the family business gives way to the corporation, this father-to-child, years-long apprenticeship will disappear as a form of learning in society. A person will become a mechanic the way one becomes nearly anything else in modern life: through formal training and certification.

The rationalization of repair leads to repairing that is similar to modern assembly. In a typically rationalized repair a mechanic removes a part of the machine thought to be defective and puts another in its place. Because automobiles are owned for fewer years, the work of replacing parts is not complicated by rusty bolts or deteriorated mounting brackets. It is a simple procedure, detailed in manuals. The defective parts are seldom repaired. In fact in many of the components (particularly the ignition systems) of modern cars, internal elements are sealed and impossible to fix.

These repairs are done "by the book," a manual that specifies not only procedures but also hourly rates for specific jobs. There are tools designed for specific repairs, but their expense and limited usefulness make it difficult for any but the largest garages to buy them.

What appears to be the final stage of this evolution of repair is computer-assisted troubleshooting. Automobiles are increasingly designed so they can be plugged into a computer in a repair shop; two computers, one on board and one off, communicate to diagnose the maladies of the automobile. The repairman reads a computer printout and replaces parts on its instructions. The process of repair has become simple, but the knowledge of the repairman in relation to the system he or she repairs is very limited. Repair has become deskilled in much the same way as the work of assembly. The method of repair has come to resemble a familiar contour of society—experts are specialized but do not command knowledge that integrates what they know with the "larger picture." They become, in fact, subordinate to machines—in this case computers. They have eliminated intuition, the integrative, imaginative, and detailed objectivity, and replaced it with a consciousness of routine—the limited inductiveness of repair through parts changing. This evolution is reflected in the remarks of Hugh Lickiter, a seventy-six-year-old retired blacksmith, who stated: "We don't do anything right down to the scratch and we don't have real mechanics anymore, we have parts men. They take off one part and put another on. Now there are machines that determine what is the matter with other machines and I just don't know about it. There used to be a type of work that a man took pride in his ability to see it through but now one man does this, another man that, and when it's finished, no one knows what he's done nor has any authority about it. A man has no interest but in pay day and quitting time" (Baskin 1976, 66).

Choice diminishes for the consumer as the price of repair increases dramatically. This is partly due to the cost of the new repair machines. (In the past the repairman owned nearly all the tools he used, and they might be very limited. When I was growing up it was said that you could do an engine job on any General Motors car with a nine-sixteenths wrench and a screwdriver.) Customers, ironically (because it is not necessarily in their best interests), also come to view repair as the replacement of a part. In the past they probably accepted the judgment of the mechanic who fixed an old part, maybe only by cleaning or adjusting. But customers now expect that repairs will be expensive and equate the quality of the solution with the cost and number of new parts installed. The distrust of the mechanic who cleans and files a small part and suggests a bit of preventive maintenance is similar to the attitude of patients who demand that the doctor do something dramatic to relieve their malaise. In a subtle way consumers, as well as repairmen, come to have their consciousness defined by the technique. Consumers find themselves more willing to accept the dictates of the computer than the concrete and "fallibly attuned" knowledge of the repairman.[12]

All of these elements of rationalized repair can be contrasted with how Willie learned, how he teaches, and how he works.

Learning and Teaching

In the beginning of Willie's working life, cars were still a recent addition to American culture. The life of Willie's father, a blacksmith, began in the horse age and ended only a few years after the widespread adoption of the automobile. Horses remained the main engine in farm work, however, coexisting with and gradually giving way to the tractor for—depending on the region of the country—three or four decades after the introduction of the automobile. It was not until the decade following the Second World War that the last teams in American agriculture were retired, and these changes were put off ten to fifteen more years in most parts of Europe. The farrier/blacksmith, then, was a holdover from an earlier era at the same time as he became an important part of the new age.

Willie's father was one of these transitional figures, with one foot in the horse-driven age and one in the engine age. Willie relates:

"A blacksmith in my father's day, along with shoeing horses, did blacksmith's welds—he built the parts for machinery—well, almost the same principle as

I'm doing now. It would be a garage and a blacksmith's shop at the same time. My father worked on cars as well as doing blacksmith's work: '31, '32—that's as far back as I can remember. When I'd get home in the evenings from school I'd have to stand on a box to help turn the forge. I was seven years old."

This was part of a life, Willie says, where "there were not that many things you owned that you didn't make." Even if you did buy something you couldn't make, preparing it for use often required handwork:

"You would buy a gun, then take it to a gunsmith who would make the parts fit. A lot of gunsmiths made their own parts for a handcrafted gun. There was no such thing as manufacturing identical pieces. They were tooled by a blacksmith. The gun barrel, for instance, was drilled."

In addition:

"When you bought a car, especially the Model T's, you got a wrench kit with it to adjust your bearings and everything else with. Your bearings were all shimmed. You'd pull a little base pan off the bottom to adjust your bearings. You did most of that yourself. But a lot of people didn't know enough about mechanical work, so they'd take it to the blacksmith's shop. Some of the people had regular little car shops set up, but not many. I believe that more people understood machines back then. They knew more of the fundamentals of them—how they were supposed to operate—than they do now. Now a person goes to school and just learns just what they're teaching them there—he learns nothing on his own from his parents because their parents don't have any interest in it."

Willie's father dealt with basic problem solving: getting machines back to work. This was especially necessary when fixing agricultural machinery; farming had to be done when the time was ripe. In this setting a worker comes to view nearly all machine breakdowns as repairable simply because the practical necessities demand that the repair be done.

It was, then, the blacksmith who became the first auto mechanic, as he had been the farm equipment repairman. Their auto work was often similar to the work they did in repairing farm machines: fixing broken metal or making new pieces. What seems unusual in Willie's work, repairing broken parts and fashioning new ones, has been carried over from his father's work as a blacksmith. Willie has extended that knowledge to new technologies and even now makes many of the parts used in his repairs.

The contrast between the two methods of repair—the formal and the informal or the rationalized and the nonrationalized—is etched in the pattern of learning skills and passing them on. Willie learned from his father in the daily practice of a small shop. In his words:

"When my father was doing something I was eager; I was watching him. Maybe the next time I'd have to do it for him. But I watched him do it the first time. That made a lot of difference too.

"My father was a guy who didn't have much patience for teaching someone. If he sent you out to do something—that's it—you went out and did it. If you didn't know how, you learned how. Kids now don't get that pushed on them. So they don't learn anything from their parents."

It is perhaps easy to idealize such an arrangement, especially since parents' work is now so seldom passed on to children in a family context. The learning, however, was not always gentle or easy. The child's work was part of the work of the family and carried a lot of responsibility. Punishment for mistakes was as natural as the responsibility. Yet Willie characterizes what perhaps looks like a rather severe relationship between adult and child as a bond of interest and commitment. Recall Willie's earlier statement that now people learn only at school; that parents are less interested in their children than they were in the past. Willie speaks of his own childhood:

"My father always figured that you did something, and did it wrong, that was one lesson you learned. If you got kicked and sent back to do it again, you'd try to do it right because you're never going to forget the first time you did it wrong. My father always said: 'If you learned the hard way, you learned for good.' My grandfather was the same way."

Willie teaches his children similar methods in a similar setting. His son, now in his late twenties, grew up working with and learning the principles of repair at home. Willie recalls:

"When a car would come in, or a piece of farm machinery—our main work was farm machines when Skip was growing up—he was watching me. I'm hard of hearing so I use a stethoscope on the engines. I'd show him with a stethoscope—show him the different sounds—I showed him how to pick out those sounds. I was picking it up with the stethoscope, but he could take the stethoscope off and he could hear the sound, easier than I could.

"I taught him the sounds of different kinds of bad ignition. If a valve is skipping, or burned, it would sound different in the exhaust. Or if you pull the coil wire and turn the engine over you can tell if you've got a burned valve. It'll hiss through the exhaust. If it's burnt real bad you'll get the same thing when it's running at slow speed. On your tractors you can pick it up very distinctly because you can idle them right down to about a hundred rpm—you can hear every cylinder just about. If you learn mechanicking on farm equipment the automotive comes 100 percent easier."

Welding was taught in a similar way:

"When Skip was young," Willie begins, "I had a blacksmith's shop out here with my regular shop. He learned a little about it—that's where he learned how to weld. When he was about seven years old he set out here at the old blacksmith's shop—one day he struck up a bead and went across a piece of metal with it. When he stopped he threw the helmet back, looked at it, 'Humph!—that's as good as Frenchie's.' The guys sitting here busted right out laughing—they went over and looked at it, and they agreed with him! Well, nowadays you don't get the opportunity, actually. When I was teaching him all this—Billy and Mike Murphy—they were always around, and getting right into the same deal. Billy Murphy turned out to be a damned good mechanic, and a good welder—and Mike—he's a good mechanic—he works for Niagara Mohawk. They all grew up together, like brothers."

Of Willie's two girls the younger, now a preteenager, is a fixture in the shop. She hovers about Willie as he works, anticipating which tools he'll need and having them ready before he asks for them. She can guess the size of a wrench or socket better than most adult mechanics. She has picked up the shop lingo—frustration over stuck nuts or recalcitrant snap rings—and when she uses some of the sexually connotative expressions that link tools to functions of the body it is very humorous because of her innocence. She has become one more voice badgering Willie to help her out when she gets into a problem she cannot solve. She does projects of her own—rebuilding bicycles, making trailers, or repairing lawn mowers. Willie gives her jobs she is capable of—disassembling small engines, sanding surfaces to be painted, cleaning up machines to be worked on. She understands the rhythms of the shop and fits in completely. She helps people who are working on their own projects and often knows where esoteric tools have landed. One can sense that by her late teens she will have become a very competent mechanic. In just the way Willie's son Skip gained his reputation as a me-

4 Julie repairing her bicycle in anticipation of spring.

chanic, so will Julie. One wonders what form her entrance to a traditionally male occupation will take.

Willie also teaches anyone who comes to the shop who is willing to be taught. The shop becomes a school, and to get work done you must often become a student. This was made strikingly clear the first time I came there in need of help. I nursed my car—which was running terribly and smelling of gasoline—to the shop well after what I expected to be closing hours. A quick look showed gas leaking from the carburetor; I was lucky not to have burned up the car driving it to the shop. Willie, whom I had met but once before, looked the engine over briefly and told me to disassemble the linkages and gas lines. I had no tools in my car; he told me to use his by simply pointing at the rack in the corner of the shop. He kept busy with his own work, but I could see that he watched me out of the corner of his eye. When I had extracted the faulty piece he made a new fitting and gently tapped it into the carburetor. He then found a piece of used gas line to replace a section that was rotted and broken. After I reassembled the linkages he adjusted the carburetor and timed the distributor, asking as he worked, "Do you hear that now? . . . Listen while I turn this . . . hear how it goes in and out of tune." I arrived with what I think is the typical mentality of a customer: fearful of the after-hours shop rate, wondering about the honesty and competence of the mechanic, and hoping he would fix my car. What I encountered was a man cheerfully willing to offer a stranger the use of his tools, then to stop his work to finish mine and make a part to complete my repair. I think the charge was a couple of dollars and the invitation to return later that evening to play country and western music.

Because of the way the shop is run, it becomes more like a public than a private space. Not everyone, however, shares the use of the shop and the tools. If you are interested and willing to learn, and if Willie has sensed that you will handle the tools properly, you are invited to use them. People work on their jobs (with Willie's tools) until they get stuck and then seek Willie's help. Customers help each other as well, often lending a hand while waiting for Willie to help them. Everyone who works there seems to pick up the rhythm of cooperative work and grade themselves into skill levels, helping others on lower levels. Willie often goes from project to project, focusing on the difficult problem in a long process, then moving on to another. He teaches, jokes, encourages. Customers compete for Willie's attention to move their own projects ahead. In this way, as Willie works he teaches.

In these photographs Willie has retrieved a wheel puller, a tool used to remove a car or trailer wheel, for a customer (my wife, in fact) who is about to repack the wheel bearings on her horse trailer (5, 6).

WILLIE "I was explaining to her that you have got to use a hammer on it, and when you do you've got to really rap it. You don't tap it—you rap it. Hard. Because if you don't you mess the tool up. If you hit it gentle you just burr the places where you are supposed to hit it. She was wondering what to do with it—she'd never pulled a wheel before."

DOUG: "You'll stop what you're doing and get a tool that's worth a lot of money and then explain to someone how to use it—you'll put it into somebody's hands who has never used it before."

WILLIE: "This wheel puller is sturdy, it's strong, all you've got to do is use a little strength on it. But you've got to hit it in the right place. You hit the end wrench that fits over the hex head; you hit it sideways to spin the shaft against the center of the wheel. If you hit the end you see sticking out on 6 you'll rivet the wrench right on. A person can *very* easily mess this up. But I think she has a kind of knowledge—a mechanical knowledge that comes to her when she is doing things like that. The average person you don't hand a tool like that to."

DOUG: "That day there were five people trying to get your attention; just taking your tools and using them, bringing them back, looking for parts—it's like a community shop!"

5 Willie retrieves a wheel puller for a customer working on her own project.

6 Willie hands the wheel puller to the customer and explains how to use it.

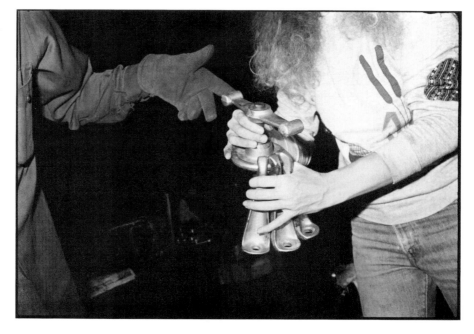

WILLIE: "You know, that's something I've never seen anywhere else, where they come in—three or four people—a lot of them know each other. While I'm doing a job for one person, another person, if he has something to take apart—they will all pitch in and do it! Somebody will be wanting to change a tire, and someone else will know how to use the tire changer, so they'll help them out."

DOUG: "When I first came up here it frustrated me. I was impatient to get my job done."

WILLIE: "How well I know! Curt was the same way. I slowed him way down. And Motor Mouth! He used to be running all the time when he first came here! He has slowed down a good 75 or 80 percent from what he used to be. I'd jump him right in front of his wife for that. He'd turn to say something to me, and then she'd get on him. He'd actually run! He didn't walk from one place to another, he ran. A lot of them are like that; after a while they slow down, they help each other, and eventually I get to them, too."

Disassembling Intuition

Willie's knowledge can be thought of as intuitive instead of rationally objective. But "intuitive" may just be used to name something that is not easy to understand. "Intuitive," I think, really applies to a more detailed objectivity, called into play in a freer and more imaginative manner. In the following studies of Willie's work, I have looked at how his understanding—"intuitive" or simply objective in a more detailed manner—is embodied in methods and kinds of knowing.

The basis of Willie's working knowledge is his deep understanding of many materials. It is knowing how metal, wood, plastic, or even paper and cardboard respond to attempts to alter their shape, density, or pliability. The knowledge is so detailed it leads to engineering: forming materials into machines or correcting design problems in the process of repair. Fixing and making are often very close together on the continuum of Willie's working knowledge, both grounded in a basic knowledge of the materials.

Willie learned about metal in his father's blacksmith shop. At the forge a person comes to understand metal in a fine and detailed way, through heavy handwork, altering metal with heat and then reforming it with the hammer and the cold of water or ice. Willie explains:

"In a manner of speaking the blacksmith was a machinist. Everything was molded and drilled. When it came to farm machinery, when you had a broken part—

usually it was steel—very little cast [iron] used at that time—you'd use what they call a 'blacksmith's weld' to weld them back. You'd get your metals to a certain temperature and then put the two pieces together and hammer them. You'd hammer them right back into one piece. If you wanted to weld two pieces together, you would heat one piece and work it out longer. You can stretch metal by working it. And do the same for the other piece, but do it the opposite way. You make each piece so it overlaps the other one. Then they had a—some of them used it and some of them didn't—they had a flux that they dipped them into. They'd put them in the forge and get them to almost melting hot, they'd dip it in the flux, slap it together and start hammering. A forge could be as big as this tabletop—it would have a three-, four-foot top. But you had a small pot in the center where it heated. Take the two pieces and band them together when they're almost melting hot. You judge that by color. You had to know your temperatures and you had to know your metals to do a blacksmith's weld. You've got to know the same things for gas welding—which metals will weld together and which ones won't. Each type of metal has its own heat range. Well, you had to do the same thing with your forge—you had to use a different heat range for different metals. You altered the amount of time you left it in the forge. If you get to white hot—the next step is melting. If you go too far you start all over again! You had to have an eye for it."

Tempering metal, adjusting its hardness or pliability with heat and cold, was a procedure similar to welding. Like welding, it depended on the eye as well as the hand. Willie explains:

"When you were tempering something you get it to what they call a cherry red. One piece of steel you might need to get to a cherry red, maybe another one a little redder. You cool it in certain ways as you go along. It draws the temper into the steel. Makes it harder. But if you cool it too quickly it gets tempered so hard it's just like glass—you can break it.

"They have what they call flame temper, an oil temper, or a water temper. Like if you sharpen a pick—you hammer the point out on a pick and then you want to temper it so it won't burr over when you hit a stone—that's a cherry temper. But if you temper it *too* hard and you hit a stone, it'll pop the end right off. You dip it in the water slow. And it'll turn a bluish color as the temper works out into it. And your coal temper—a temper out of a coal forge—is a lot better than your gas temper. See, they use gas forges now. Or I can temper with a torch, but you've got to be very careful with it. When you're using gas you're only heating one side at a time. When you're using coal you're poking the metal right into the hot ashes. It heats it more evenly, all the way through and around. Where with your gas you don't get that. And you only heat one side with the torch, and it's not as good."

Learning about metal through the blacksmith's techniques became, for the first generation of welders, the basis for gas welding. These welders, like Willie, could understand welding because they understood metal in a deeper and more fundamental way than welders who learn first with the torch. The progress at the forge was slow, the changes in the metal relatively gradual, all controlled by hand. The blacksmith's weld is an extension of forming, bending, and adapting metal. Gas welding, which evolved from the blacksmith's techniques, is a more efficient method of cutting and binding metal that, for basic work, requires less knowledge. The gas welder is a tool that can change metal relatively easily and very quickly. The operator of a gas welder, to do crude work, need know only the basics of how to use the tool. On the other hand, a modern welder who learned his or her trade as a blacksmith summons a detailed and many-sided knowledge that refines the use of the technique.

Traditional bodywork—straightening bent metal on automobiles, for example, depended upon techniques similar to those of the blacksmith. The traditional "body man" reformed metal rather than filling in dents with body fill, an epoxy compound that is applied to metal and then sanded to shape. Filling in dents with epoxy is relatively simple, but if the area being filled is large the repair may not be permanent. Traditional body men like Willie use epoxy compound for final, surface corrections after the large bends and dents in the metal have been re-formed. Willie explains the connection between the two:

"The things I learned working with my dad in the blacksmith's shop, about how metal acts when it's heated up and cooled off—that's part of body and fender work. You can move metal any way you want to with bodywork. You can use heat to shrink metal, or you can use heat to expand metal. Ice, water . . . you've seen me use ice. I don't think you've seen me use heat. I've got a hammer up there they call a 'shrinking hammer.' It's knurled. One end of it is square and it's full of knurls. And it makes those knurls right into the metal. The other end is round with the same type of knurls in it. I don't use it very often. It actually draws the metal together. . . . They don't do that kind of bodywork any more—they use body fill."

The traditional method of bodywork involved not only different hand techniques, but a view of the mass of metal as an interconnected, interpendent entity:

"[To work metal this way] you do one thing at a time, but you're always thinking of the project as a whole and how it's being affected by what you're doing. You might have a dent on the top of the fender, but you don't work on it there—you work on it on the bottom, to draw it out. Most people don't see that you're working on it if you're not pounding right on it where you can see the dent. You never start bringing out the big bump first. You bring it out the way it went in. And it will come out 100 percent better. If you start pushing the big bump out first—on a fender, or a quarter panel, or something like that—you'll be leaving all this little crinkly stuff around that will be harder to work out later on. Where if you start working it out the way it came in it goes better."

These skills make the work of fixing and fashioning part of the same basic technique:

"A blacksmith could take a sheet of metal and do anything with it he wants to," Willie says. "If he's a *blacksmith*. We used to take a sheet of metal and make fenders—during World War II, when you couldn't get parts. We made Cadillac fenders, Chevrolet fenders; front ones, back ones—it didn't matter. We'd just take a sheet of metal; mold it. Heat and the hammer. All you had for a mold was the look of the one fender that was sitting there. You shaped it to that."

Material is pushed and bent, heated and cooled, pounded and twisted. Knowledge of the materials allows Willie to redefine the fixability of objects. It also lets him adopt the perspective of the engineer who designed the machine, to redesign as a part of repair. Examples of this kind of work follow.

Making a Water Bend

The machine Willie repairs in this example is a *blower*—a piece of farm equipment used to transfer silage from a wagon into a silo. The blower looks like the propeller of an airplane inside a casing. Several heavy bars radiate from a central shaft. On the end of the bars are paddles that actually push the material through the blower and shoot it through a long tunnel running up the side of the silo. The blower runs at high speed, since it is sometimes necessary to blow the silage a hundred feet to the top.

"This blower got bent by one of Tom Rogers's men," Willie begins, "when he ran a ten-ton hydraulic jack through it. He was working on it, and he laid the jack right on the intake of the blower. He started it up, and that's what hap-

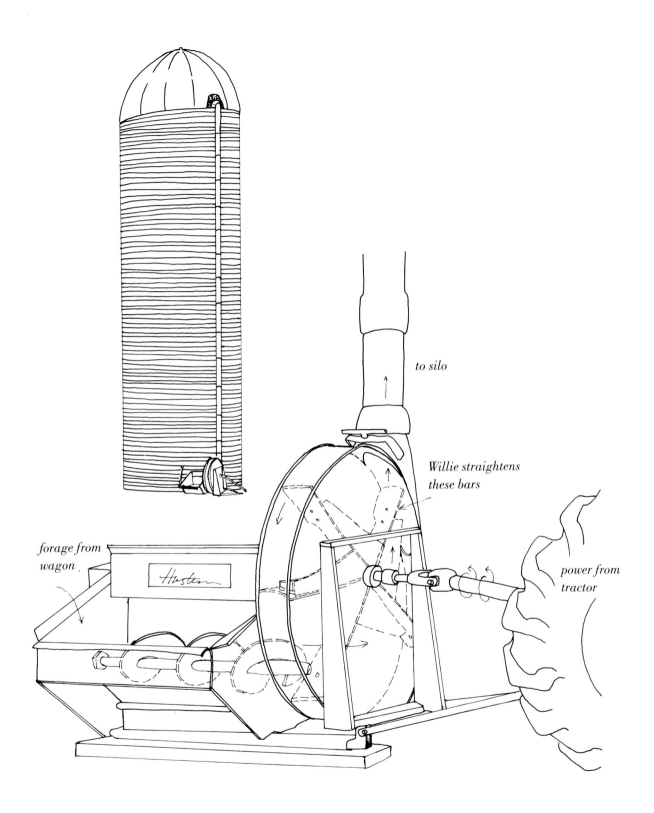

to silo

*Willie straightens
these bars*

*forage from
wagon*

*power from
tractor*

7 A silo blower.

8 Willie attaches an extension to the arm of the blower with a large C-clamp. He will mount the Porta-Power—a portable hydraulic jack—to the end of the extension to twist the arm of the blower.

pened. The blower drew it in because it's got rollers that push everything into it. It bent every paddle in it. Bent all the arms; as you can see, there's quite a twist in the arms.

"First (8) you put the leverage on it. I put a piece of metal on it to extend it so I can jack it back in place with the Porta-Power. You can't get the jack on the arm itself, so you twist it with the Porta-Power, as you can see in 9. You've got to be careful the Porta-Power doesn't slip out. There's a little V in the bottom of the Porta-Power—you can set it over a piece of metal and it won't slip one way or another, and you block the wheel so it can't turn."

"I'm heating the twist to bring it out, as you see in photographs 10 and 11. You can't just bend it without heating it. It's too heavy. Then I use the water to cool it (12); it helps bring it back more. The speed you pour the water depends on how much you're bending it. It was bent off to the side—it doesn't show that well in the photographs—it was bent around and away from the cover. I twisted it up with the Porta-Power, but it left too much metal on the backside of the bar, so I'm shrinking the metal on the one side to get it straight. So when I put the water on it, it cooled it faster and shrank it on that side—that's a 'water bend'. You don't always use heat to bend. You use cold water, ice, or whatever you've got. In the winter I just go out and pick up some ice to use.

"I drew that about three-sixteenths of an inch in a distance of about eight inches. I had to heat it on both sides to get the twist out, but I only put the water on one side.

"The heat is the most important thing when you're straightening. You've got to heat the right places so it will bend back where it is bent. The heat *relaxes* the metal so you can bend it. Here I'm using an acetylene torch, but I'm not using it full power. I heat it to color, and the color I bring it to depends on the heft of the metal. There's a range of colors, from white hot to cherry red."

"This blower was considered junk," Willie continues. "Tom traded it to George Weikoff, the dealer, and Bill Nash looked at it; took me down to look at it to see if I could fix it for him. Other people looked at it—they said it was too far gone to fix. They didn't have enough patience. Every one of those bars has to be bent exactly the same way. And they had welded the shaft in place, that's not supposed to be welded. It's supposed to be a slip shaft so it can be taken apart to disassemble the machine. I fixed that too. And when I finished I balanced the bars. Most people don't do that. I added weld to lighter bars until it was balanced perfectly. When it runs it sounds just like a fan—no vibration."

9 Willie pumping the Porta-Power to twist one arm of the blower.

10 Willie heats the arm of the blower with an acetylene torch so it will "take" the twist.

11 Heating the blower bar (close-up).

12 Pouring water on the metal to make a water bend.

Building a Stove Door

In the following passage I study how Willie's knowledge of materials contributes to his engineering skills. Willie is building the door for a wood furnace, to finish a heating system for my wife's solar greenhouse. Homemade stoves are common in the North Country, but most are roughly made and inefficient. Willie's designs, on the other hand, are engineered for specific purposes. Draft, interior space, and chimney dimensions must all be integrated into the design. The stove Willie designed for the greenhouse is double walled, with a blower that forces cool air into two openings cut into the lower part of the sides. The air is heated between the walls of the stove and then forced out an opening in the top to be distributed to planting beds, heat-storage chambers, or wherever in the greenhouse hot air is needed.

The stove was finished in the middle of a difficult winter. Although here I am interested in the relation between engineering and a deep knowledge of materials, I have included some of the circumstances that surrounded this job because they show how the seasons affect Willie's working life. His ability to design a wood stove comes in part from his own experience at managing the seasons.

Willie had made the stove, except for the door, two summers before. Finishing the door became one of the jobs that just didn't get done—we used the stove with a makeshift door while Willie kept promising to get to it. Finally in midwinter of the second year we broke the stove off its cement pad in the greenhouse, lugged it up the stairs, rolled it through the knee-deep snow to the car, and drove it to the shop.

It was a time of great difficulty around Willie's shop and house. Willie was suffering from lingering flu and recurrent immobility from an old industrial accident. In the fall he had worked hard getting his house finished enough to live in, and he'd had little time to cut firewood. By midwinter his supply had run out, and we were in the midst of a twenty-five below zero cold spell that lasted and lasted. Firewood had to be hauled from the woods every day with a snowmobile and sled. The sled held only a few armloads, which went directly into the house and usually into a waiting fire in one of Willie's homemade stoves. The cold took its toll on the chain saws and the snowmobile; breakdowns were frequent. The snow in the woods was waist deep, and the snowmobile kept getting buried. On the other hand, the early snow had kept the ground from freezing hard enough to get the Jeep into the woods. So energy was focused on the subsistence effort of keeping warm and maintaining the machines that ensured that warmth. And at twenty-five below zero the inefficiency of the small machines was dramatic—back and forth with the snow

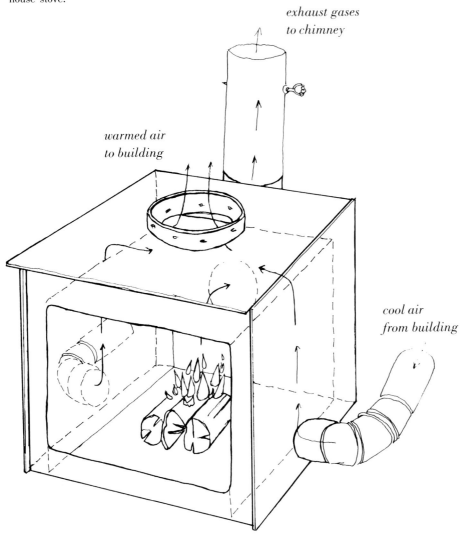

13 Diagram of the green-house stove.

exhaust gases to chimney

warmed air to building

cool air from building

machine, back and forth—never getting very much ahead, even with consider-able work.

Not much was happening in the shop, which slowed the money flow to a trickle and aggravated the difficulties brought on by the cold. Sparing wood to heat the shop was itself an issue. And even with the two stoves in the shop going full blast the temperature seldom rose to a comfortable working level.

As Willie's flu finally receded, we arranged a day to make the door. It was a typically difficult winter day. I arrived in the morning; we spent forty-five minutes moving wood and lighting wood stoves in both ends of the shop. Several of Willie's friends arrived, all with their own problems that required Willie's solutions. Willie paused to work on Green's truck starter. Clyde Henry wanted help on his Ford trac-tor. Frank's bursitis had advanced until he could no longer gather his wood; Willie filled the trunk of Frank's old Chevy with some logs he said were too punky to use in

14 The greenhouse stove, with door parts waiting to be put together.

15 Clamping the mitered iron channel, part of the air seal, to the stove door.

16 Detail: the stove door seal.

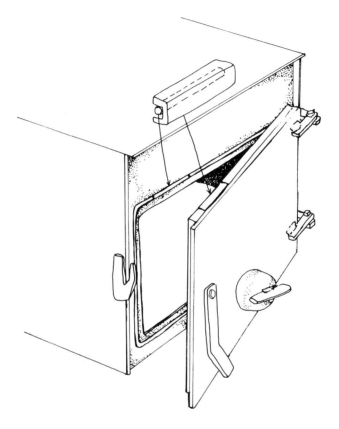

his own stoves. Of course they weren't; it was only a way to discount his generosity. After the long morning of preparation Pauline, Willie's wife, fed everyone stew made from a rabbit a neighbor had brought the day before. Finally, in the early afternoon, we returned to the shop and focused our attention on the stove door. Once begun the job, so long delayed, proceeded smoothly.

WILLIE: "The design of this stove was from the one I built for my cellar. The one for the greenhouse, that we're making here, is quite a bit larger—more efficient for a greenhouse—it'll hold a fire longer. But made on the same principle. If you don't have this type of a seal [see 16], you'd stand a chance of sparks coming out between the door and the stove. The door will warp a little when it heats, causing a gap, and it'll come back when it cools.

"When you heat one side of metal [as happens when you use the stove]—it's just like taking a dry board and making it wet on one side—it'll make it bow the other way. So the channel and bead we welded on the stove is a seal *and* a spark arrester.

17 Willie welds the channel to the door.

18 Willie welds the door. The reinforcing-rod seal sitting on top of the stove will be welded onto the front of the stove so that the channel closes over it.

"The channel is welded on the door, and we laid the seal, which is the re-rod [half-inch steel reinforcing rod], into the door when we were welding it into a square to make sure we got it the right size. Then the re-rod was welded onto the stove.

"I remember this square piece of welded channel laid around the shop for about a year," I say. "I've got a photo taken a year before showing you using it to line up the side pieces of a trailer you were making."

Willie laughs, "Yeah, I used it for a straightedge!"

He studies the photos:
"If the piece I'm welding on isn't accurate the door won't close properly. But all this is the easiest welding there is—the long bead. You clamp the pieces and just run your rod along and let it flow in. Biggest problem a lot of people have is that they get in too big a hurry. The more time you take the better weld you get. The slower you move with the rod, the heavier the weld. If you move too fast it's what some people call bubblegum welding. I told you about that before. You just get bubbles of metal on it. You go so fast it doesn't blend together. It just lays there in beads as it comes off the rod. See, as your metal heats it comes off the rod in droplets. It doesn't pour off there like most people think it does. If you're not hot at the spot where that's dropping off—where it's molten metal—it cools off too quick and just lays there in a bead. You can see it with the dark mask on. But if you go too slow you can burn a hole in the metal you're welding, depending on its thickness and heat range.
"There's a problem on this weld because I'm welding light metal against heavy metal. You hold the rod a certain way to get a good bead, and you can't hold it as heavy on light metal as you can on heavy metal. So you've got to go accordingly. You can see the heat as you're working; you can see how it's blending. You're watching the colors of the two metals; you're watching it blend. That's why when you see someone welding, even if he's doing a tedious little job—you won't hear him talking. He's concentrating on his metals. Because if he doesn't, he hasn't got a weld that will hold up."

I say, "You got that welded and you set it upright next to the stove to let it cool. I looked at it and said, 'my God, it's warped—it's not going to seal!' Frank and Raymond are back there by the stove keeping warm. They walked over, wrinkled up their foreheads, and said, 'I guess you really did fuck that one up, Willie! His door ain't going to seal!'"

19 The warped door viewed
from the edge. The channel is
welded to the right side. The
door leans up against the stove,
here viewed from the front.
Note the bow in the edge of
the door facing the front.

20 Using an eight-pounder to
straighten the door.

Willie answers, "Yeah, quite a bend in it. Heat bend. When you weld two pieces of metal that are different thickness together, the one that's lighter cools faster, and it draws the other one. It drew the door in a rainbow shape—the lighter metal actually bent the heavier. So it had to be straightened to be used. And if you could straighten it without heating it she'd never warp back. With a wood fire the two metals heat together and evenly—it's not like throwing a torch or an arc [welder] on it. The whole area heats up instead of just that small spot. I might have been able to straighten it by leaving it clamped when it was cooling off. But on this we didn't use clamps. There's a quarter-inch or more bow in that!"

"To bend it back I clamped the door to the big iron to hold it steady, so it wouldn't bounce off on my feet, and used the hammer on it. An eight-pounder. It took about half an hour, as I remember, but it was flat when I was finished."

"I was surprised you could take that little bit of a bend out of that big an area by pounding on it," I say, "God, you made a racket."

"You can take metal and work it just like you take sandpaper and work wood. But you do it with a hammer on metal. You figure—that was a two-foot span, and we're taking a quarter-inch out of three-eighths stock. Plus you've got to figure the metal welded onto it. It wouldn't mess up the channel because it was laying flush. If it wouldn't have been laying flush, on flat metal, it would have messed it up when you hit it. But it was laying flush enough that it worked out. You work with metal long enough, you know just about what you can do with it. This is like a blacksmith's work—you've got the same thing right here, straightening that door. Only thing, I did it cold instead of with heat. If I'd done it with heat I'd put the heat on the opposite side from where it's laying now. You would have heated it, put a small thickness of metal under both ends, and clamped it. And when it cooled off she'd probably come back to the shape you'd wanted it. Or you'd have to raise the ends of it because it would pull some of the bow back if you didn't. You'd have to go just beyond the point of straight. About an eighth of an inch. You'd need about a sixteenth of an inch on each end. But what I like about working with a hammer—you know where you've got to hit by looking at it. If you hit it hard enough, and if your iron is solid enough that you've got it laying on, she's going to move where you want it to move—not where *it* wants to move. You'll find the same thing hammering a saw for a sawmill. If a saw gets a lot of warp in it you don't take it someplace and have it straightened, you take it somewhere and have it hammered. You can hammer a warp right out of it by stretching the outer edge of the warp. If you've got a bow you generally hammer the outer edge, or sometimes the inner edge—whatever you need to get the warp out. You *pull* the metal. If you've got a bulge in the metal of your car and you want to shrink it—you don't hit it on the top of the bulge. You heat it—use water and shrink it. Bring it right back in. But if the bulge is too big you take a dolly on the inside and use a hammer on the outside as you heat around it and work it right back in. You can take a bulge right out of it. *You* want to hit the mountain—get it down there faster. But you can't do that. You've got to bring it down easy, work around it, work the metals in flat. Otherwise it would just wrinkle it up. Well, it's the same principle with this. When it cooled off it shrunk the metal. I had to bring it back, and the only way to bring it back was to expand it by hammering it. If you hammered enough you could hammer a bow into it in the other direction. It's like making something out of brass—it's done with a hammer. Here you are stretching two pieces of metal. The lighter one, the channel, would stretch easier than the heavy part. So you hit the heavy part, not the light part. There'd be no problem stretching the channel because that was light enough to stretch. The clamp was just to hold the metal on the iron. You don't clamp a bend out of metal that size—you work it out."

"That's on the drill press," Willie says, "drilling the openings in the door for the air to get to the fire—you just make a circle the size of the draft control and fit as many holes as you can into the circle. You keep the oil to it and it goes easier. I thought you were holding that door for me."

I comment, "I think the guy who brought the parts you used for the draft covers was holding it."

"Autry. He brought those pieces from his job—they're covers used to weld over the end of pipes. They make good dampers—I wish I could get more. And I wish I could find some more gloves like that. They're a special thermo—I can't buy them anywhere anymore."

21 Willie drills air holes in the door.

22 Damper holes. Willie will thread the center hole so the damper can be screwed in or out, regulating the amount of air blowing through the holes into the fire.

23 Willie cuts threads in the center hole with the air wrench. He has just threaded the hole in the damper, which is in the right foreground. He will weld bolt stock (cut from a long piece of threaded rod) into the damper, which can then be screwed into the door. With the damper turned in tight to the door, the fire is starved for air and burns more slowly. With the damper turned away from the door, the fire gets more oxygen and burns hotter.

WILLIE: "The hole in the center is to thread for your draft control. I started the threads with the big crescent; I finished them off with the air wrench that walks them right down through. I always figure you've got a little better job that way, too. You get quite a torque [with the air wrench], but I think it's easier on the tap [the tool that cuts the threads] with that steady torque than it is twisting that tap in with a big crescent. The taps are hard metal and they're easy to break.

"You can see the draft control in the photo; we've already drilled it and run threads through it."

Building a wood stove involves knowledge of the material it is made of, but designing one also requires knowledge of how things burn. You have to know how air behaves when it is heated and cooled. The air flow into and out of the stove—controlled by the damper and the chimney—regulates the rate at which the wood burns, the intensity of the heat, and the ability of the fire to hold for eight to ten hours. With the completed door in place the next spring, the stove had seemed starved for air. Fires had been hard to light and maintain. I thought the stove had not been designed with adequate draft. As we study the photographs I tell Willie: "You should hear that draw through those holes. It could probably use another draft just like that one."

But in Willie's eyes the problem involves a less obvious solution. "If you get too much of a draft," Willie says, "you won't get as good a heat. You get draft where the air is *blowing* in on the fire. You need to insulate the pipe up on the roof. It was getting too cold; it wasn't drawing right. The best would be a block chimney from inside the greenhouse. Because if you have cold pipes on the out-side, or even cold pipes inside, you won't get the draft that you do if you've got the pipes heated. There's quite a vacuum to the pipe when it's heated up. It isn't really the size of the pipe. A lot of people think they have to have a real big chimney for a stove. But if you have it so that it gets the right amount of heat inside a chimney and the chimney heats right, you can get an awful draft through a small chimney. People who just put a regular pipe outside their window and up the side of their house don't get the efficiency out of their stove."

Our conversation illuminates the difference between the "quick and dirty" solution and the solution based on "deep knowledge" of materials and the natural forces that contribute to a stove's efficiency. The following summer we did build a masonry chimney in the greenhouse, and with this modification the stove worked with the efficiency Willie had described.

DOUG: "You put me on that cut—and it was going so slow. You picked up the camera and got me when I wasn't looking!" [25]

WILLIE: It was going slow because you didn't *quite* understand how to run the hacksaw.'

DOUG: "The hacksaw was dull."

WILLIE: "No, it wasn't dull—that's your imagination. You were disgusted there. Your cut was wavering off to the side because you weren't holding your saw straight and you were laying on it too hard. The harder you laid on it the less straight it would go. A hacksaw *plays* its way through the metal. You do the same thing with a handsaw cutting wood. If you lay on it too hard it will not cut on a straight line. Take your time—let it play."

DOUG: "You welded this on and I said to myself, 'What the hell is he doing?'" [28]

24 Willie: "To everyone else it looks like junk; to me it looks like stuff I can use. I was looking for something to make the hinges with."

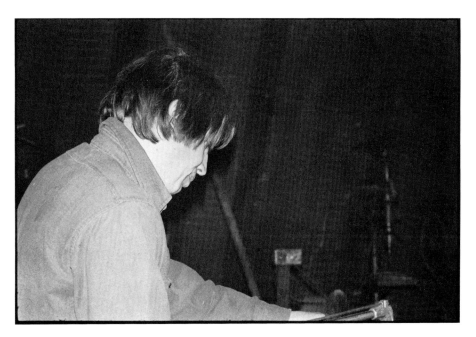

25 Cutting steel for a hinge.

WILLIE (laughs): "Yeah, it is a little ridiculous welding on a big piece, but I didn't burn my fingers holding it! That we made into the latch jaw, the piece the handle drops into."

WILLIE: "I cut a little out of the latch so it would draw up tight. I bent it a little, then cut a groove out of the backside so it would lock up against the jaw. It didn't force the door shut the way it was." [30, 31]

WILLIE: "The weather broke that next Saturday—we're finishing up—trimming and grinding—with the garage door open!" [32, 33]

The stove was completed, moved back to the greenhouse, and installed.

26 Willie positions the parts
before beginning to weld the
reinforcing rod onto the front
of the stove.

27 Welding.

28 Making the latch jaw.

29 Trimming the latch jaw.

30 "Carving" the latch jaw with the torch.

31 Willie heats the handle and bends it so that pushing it into the jaw will draw the door tighter to the stove.

32, 33 Willie grinds and trims the hinges.

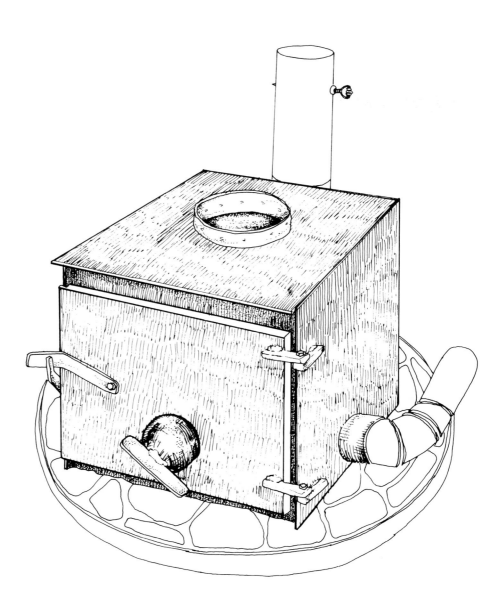

34 The finished stove.

Redesigning a Door Handle

This example shows how Willie's work involves redesigning parts that have broken or worn out. In this case the engineers who designed the early Saab 99 door handle made a few small mistakes that Willie corrected in his repair. Willie's repair includes choosing materials, for example, that are more appropriate than those used originally.

The handles were designed to be squeezed open, but the part that takes most of the pressure was made of white metal, weak where a shaft passes through on which the lever pivots. The handle was designed to move freely on small plastic ball bearings that ran in a groove between the handle and the lever. It was a good design except that the handle was open to grit and snow, so that the plastic balls eventually deteriorated and fell out. The white metal part was then not strong enough to take the pressure required to squeeze the door open. One of my door handles broke on a twenty-below morning as I tried to get into my car; the other broke when my son's 250-pound baby-sitter yanked open the passenger door.

"Yours broke like lots of them do," Willie begins as we examine the photos of a still uncompleted repair. "All you have to do is pull on them just the wrong way and it will snap the white metal piece on the inside that unlatches the door. . . . Some of it's from abuse, but it's wear too. And that piece should be made out of something heavier, something besides white metal."

"I'm thinning down the piece I made so it'll fit behind the pin in the door handle. The piece trips the latch inside the door—that's all it does. . . . You need a metal grease between those two pieces. Graphite or something to make it slip. Now it's sticking to the metal. It isn't polished enough to slide. The design is all right—it slides up and down in the handle and trips the latch. But it should be polished more so when you pull it it'll slide better. The original had a little ball in there that it rolled up and back on. With the one we made you couldn't put that plastic ball in there. The groove on the original was in the part you pulled and in the handle itself. The plastic ball was a ball bearing, to roll out and in with the latch. Now, what usually happened—that roller would get a little dirt and stuff in there, and that's when they would break. You couldn't pull it easily, and people force it and break the white metal. So I did away with the roller because the roller is what broke it before. The dirt is bound to get in there because it's all open. Saab's gone to a different handle now. The new ones have a different design; they work a lot smoother."

35 Saab door handle.

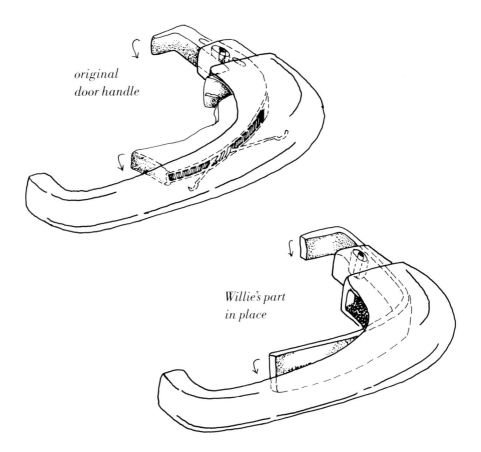

original
door handle

Willie's part
in place

36, 37 Willie makes a new part for the inside of the door handle.

38, 39 Filing and fitting the new latch.

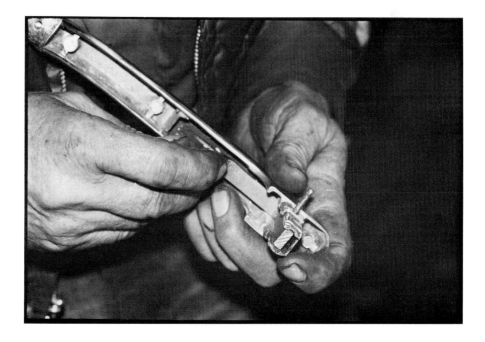

40 Chopper in operation.

Salvaging a Chopper

In the following example Willie finished restoring a blower pipe on a field chopper, a common farm implement. Photo 40 shows a chopper at work, pulled behind a tractor, shooting chopped grass into a wagon.

The repair can be looked at several ways. To begin with, the repair requires some slight reengineering. The welding itself is complex; note Willie's comments about the small details of the weld in the close-up photograph. As a result of the repair, a useless machine is made useful again; a farmer saves money and gets back to work when the season is at its peak. Finally, as happens so many times, as work is done for a customer, a small but important job is completed for a friend. Ray and P. T. sit in the background as Willie works; when the welding job on the chopper is completed, Willie turns to fixing P. T.'s chain saw muffler:

WILLIE: "You didn't get that at the beginning where I was trimming and fitting that, did you?"

DOUG: "No, when I walked up to the shop this is what you were doing. I took the photograph before you knew I'd driven in."

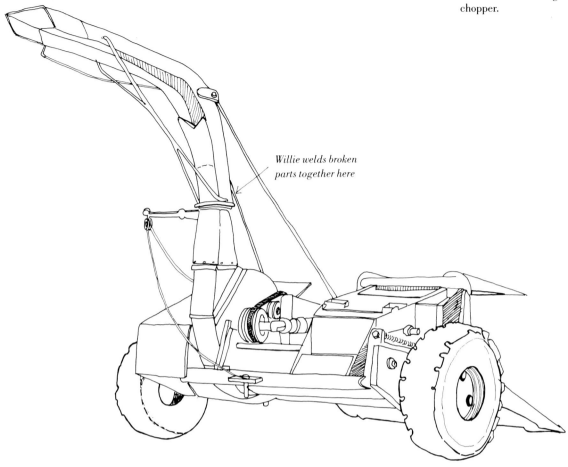

Willie welds broken parts together here

WILLIE: "That whole head part swivels. This is a blower pipe, a distributor pipe for a chopper—to blow corn [or grass] into a wagon. You pick up the ensilage with it and bring it to the barn. You got here just as I was fitting it on. See, none of this is welded up around here (points to the ragged seam on the pipe shown in 42 and 43). I was just fitting this back on there because they had cobbled it up."

DOUG: "What happened to this in the first place?"

WILLIE: "Sometimes when you're not watching closely and you go through a gully, the blower pipe will hit on the edge of the wagon, and that bends it— breaks it. The vibration will also break it—it broke this one right off. I trimmed it all down; took off all the old metal and old weld, and I had to shorten it about an inch and a half to where I could get it welded on good metal again—the inch and a half I shortened it wouldn't make that much difference. I had it setting on the drum when you came in; I was fitting it and tacking it so then I could go around and weld it.

42 Willie attaches the two parts of the blower pipe with flexible weld.

43 Willie tacks the shortened end back onto the blower pipe.

44 Willie has turned the pipe over and is working on the underside of the repair.

"This photograph [45] has things in it I didn't notice at first. This metal was rusted; eat so bad it didn't even want to acetylene weld right. To begin with, it's galvanized metal and it's hard to work with. There was quite a part that was broke out from the metal being aged so much. I filled it back in. You can see the crack there. It had to be filled in in a way so that the silage wouldn't hit it coming up through. It had to be lapped lower on the upward side—otherwise it'd catch and wear right back out. Wouldn't have done much good to fix it. On about all your farm or industrial equipment it's not just welding it together again—it's the idea of welding it so it wears right, so it will last with a lot of weld and stuff, and I had to cut it all off.

"You can see that I used different welding rod in these two places. In 45 I'm using high-tensile steel. To tack it on I use a coat hanger. The high-tensile doesn't have much flexibility. The coat hanger is more mild, more flexible. It's less apt to break afterwards. Vibrations break the higher tensile a lot easier. But I used it because I'm welding the bar that comes up the side—that's an important place that needs more strength.

"See, these marks [small horizontal cracks in the middle top of photo 45, perpendicular to the weld on the left side and to the right of the welding torch] are where there have been touches of weld before, and you can see that there are cracks right beside them. They've all got to be touched up with acetylene or they'll crack out bigger. One crack runs right over to where I was welding.

"That part would run around three hundred and something. It cost him around eighty bucks to get it fixed. But the biggest problem on this is that they will very seldom have one on hand. You've got to wait so long to get it and all that time there will be silage out there in the field going to waste, spoiling. They told him it would take about five or six weeks to get one of those. With this welding it's as good as it was when it was new; in fact it's stronger. A weld you do in a shop like this is stronger than a factory weld. A factory weld is all commercial welding— they just tack it on and let it go."

DOUG: "Here you were blowing smoke through the muffler to drive every-body nuts—to smoke us out." [47]

WILLIE: "No, I was burning the muffler out—cleaning the insides. They fill up with carbons from your oil and gas mix—the two-cycle produces more car-bon. It was filled on the inside; his chain saw wouldn't run. He was going to buy a new muffler. When I did that it burned it all out clean—just as if it was a new muffler. You can see the smoke there—that's when they got up and started moving around. Those two—they're part of the scenery." [46, 47]

45 Close-up of welding.
Willie uses high-tensile steel
rod to finish the repair.

46 Willie finishes the blower
pipe repair. Raymond and
P. T. shoot the breeze as P. T.
waits for Willie to fix his
chain saw muffler; he sits on
my tire as my car also waits
for Willie's attention.

47 Burning out the inside of the chain saw muffler.

SUMMARY

These examples show some of the ways Willie brings his understanding of materials to bear on his work. They would continue as long as one chronicled Willie's work, for the knowledge is integral to the method and gives it much of its particular character. Many of the repairs seem unremarkable, such as using a cardboard box to make a gasket or a piece of discarded plastic for a small brace. But the knowledge of material makes it possible for Willie to use the odds and ends that are in profusion around the shop—to see the value (identified as usefulness) in "junk." Willie's knowledge of materials helps him understand *why* machines have deteriorated or broken down, and it leads him to see the act of repair as remedying an engineering flaw rather than replacing a part. Finally, the knowledge of material extends to the operating environment of the things Willie makes or fixes. Knowledge of how wood burns or how air moves forms the basis of a wood stove design, just as knowledge of how metal re-forms under the hammer guides the shaping of a warped stove door.

Work as Bricolage

These examples gain more depth when viewed from the perspective of Claude Lévi-Strauss, writing about the working knowledge of people in "prior" societies. In *The Savage Mind* (1966) Lévi-Strauss calls this ongoing process of problem solving the "science of the concrete"—forming one's survival by adapting the *bricoles* of the world. *Bricolage* is making use of such bricoles—the odds and ends, the bits left over, the set of unrelated or oddly related objects. According to Lévi-Strauss the *bricoleur* is most typically found as the natural man of savage (though Lévi-Strauss prefers "prior") societies, but his method resembles that of the English odd-job man or the American jack-of-all-trades. Willie, improvising with the odds and ends that drift down to him or come through barter, is the very embodiment of Lévi-Strauss's bricoleur:

Consider him at work and excited by his project. His first practical step is retrospective. He has to turn back to an already existent set made up of tools and materials, to consider or reconsider what it contains and, above all, to engage in a sort of dialogue with it, and before choosing between them, to index the possible answers which the whole set can offer to his problem. . . .

. . . the rules of his game are always to make do with "whatever is at hand," that is to say with a set of tools and materials which is always finite and is also heterogeneous because what it contains bears no relation to the current projects or indeed to any particular project, but it is the contingent result of all the occasions there have been to renew or enrich the stock or to maintain it with the remains of previous constructions or destructions. . . .

He does not confine himself to accomplishment and execution; he "speaks" not only *with* things . . . but through the medium of things; giving an account of his personality and life by the choices he makes between limited possibilities. The bricoleur may not ever complete his purpose but he always puts something of himself into it. (1966, 21)

There are several important ideas in these passages. The bricoleur is presented first as a thinker: considering, reconsidering, always with a view to *what is available*, what is at hand. The emphasis is correctly on the mental side of the dialectical process, which Lévi-Strauss calls a dialogue.

The observation that the set of tools and materials is the sum of all previous projects, and that it will be summoned to the task at hand and enlarged once again with the materials left over from the current project, captures the sense of a shop operation and of forming one's own material world through the creative use of what simply builds up during the process of work. This of course is in contrast to the idea of assembling one's tools and materials and then adding to them to fit a preconceived and definitive plan or blueprint.

Finally, Lévi-Strauss indicates that in his work the bricoleur defines and extends himself. It is not only that the work solves material problems, but also that one's life choices take on the same characteristics as the decisions made in the course of work. It is in the replication of the means that the material work influences the mental.

Lévi-Strauss's ideas about bricolage are particularly well illustrated with several modifications and designs of machines, tools, and dwellings that Willie uses himself. This is in the spirit of the bricoleur, for the "primitive mind" worked through his own material solutions as his stock of available materials was enlarged through trade.

Resurrecting a Ford Tractor

The tractor had been part of the landscape around Willie's shop for seven years. Willie had taken it from a neighboring farmer as partial payment for a welding job. When Willie got the tractor it lacked a starter, a three-point hitch, a number of control parts, and rear wheels. When the deal was made small tractors were not much in demand, and the farmer probably regarded it as a convenient way to get rid of a machine that had been allowed to deteriorate beyond usefulness. For Willie the tractor would be handy in the woods as well as around the shop.

It had been towed to Willie's on borrowed wheels and then sat beached on some elm logs, looking more and more like a permanent part of the landscape as the years went by. Parts and materials began to pile up around and on top of the machine, nearly hiding it. "Tractor still in there?" Raymond would needle Willie as he walked past. "Yup, and it's going into the shop just as soon as I get the ———— [any of a number of jobs that went in and out over the years] out of there." For eight years the shop filled up and disgorged its jobs and projects, but the tractor remained outside. In the meantime Willie came across a set of used truck wheels that he converted for the tractor, solving a major problem in the restoration project. Then one day a berth was cleared in the shop and the tractor was towed inside, its rear wheels skidding along because the engine and clutch had seized up in the years since it had been moved. The seized engine and clutch would mean an additional and perhaps expensive addition to what Willie had expected to be a straightforward restoration. I said it was too bad, but Willie answered: "What do you expect—you leave metal alone—metal rusts!"

Clyde Henry, a man who was now and then in Willie's circle of friends, finally began the tractor repair. Clyde was a retired farmer and highway engineer with time on his hands and a little money to invest in machines to be restored and re-

sold. Clyde would be around the shop a lot for a while and then not be seen at all for months. The preceding spring he had towed an old Ford tractor of his own into the shop and was rebuilding it for resale. Clyde was not very handy, and Willie was constantly stopping what he was doing to get him onto the right track or out of a situation he couldn't figure out by himself. I remember thinking at the time that Willie was spending a lot of time and energy on another goodwill job that would bring him little in return.

It was Clyde, however, who prodded Willie to rebuild the truck wheels and pull the tractor into the space vacated by Clyde's completed job. Then he began in earnest on Willie's tractor. He removed the engine head and loosened the stuck valves with applications of 808 and the gentle tap of a ball peen hammer. He disassembled the rusted clutch and cleaned most of the rust from the disk and pressure plate and otherwise put them into working order. When the job stalled for lack of a starter and Clyde saw that Willie would wait until he got the part through a trade, he bought one himself. At the same time he bought a new exhaust system, which while not functionally necessary would make the tractor a lot more pleasant to operate. I think there were at least two motives behind his buying the new parts. Clyde was less patient than Willie at seeing the job uncompleted until a starter came up in the informal flow of parts through the shop. He wanted to finish the job. I also think he realized he owed Willie for the help and the shop space he'd used during his own long job. Willie treated the exhaust system as unexpected frosting on an unexpected cake. I could see that the tractor project was part of a give-and-take between Clyde and Willie that had gone on for years. Although Willie had not named a price for helping Clyde on his job, both knew something would have to be done to carry the relationship forward.

Other minor repairs were accomplished; small holes in the gas tank were sealed; control parts were gathered and installed. I was at the shop when the tractor was ready for its first attempt at renewed life. The engine turned over easily and fired into life, but the oil pressure gauge read zero. Willie quickly turned the engine off before it ruined itself; the old pistons and bearings were dry. Before taking the engine apart to fix the oil pump Willie added a bit more oil, trying to prime it. He started the tractor again, and people gathered around to watch the gauge move back and forth a few times and then spring to the right and hold constant. We stood there grinning as the engine ran for the first time in nearly a decade—a smooth drone. Willie carefully put the tractor into gear and released the clutch, and the machine crept ahead under its own power. He drove it back and forth a few feet, "getting some of the cobwebs out," and immediately the tractor became a working part of the operation.

A few repairs remained. The grille protecting the radiator had rusted away so the radiator was exposed to brush and low branches in the woods. The thirty-five-

year-old radiator was extremely delicate and would be hard to replace if it was ruined.

A month later, on a Saturday morning, Willie's son Skip was telling Willie over coffee that they ought to do something about the front of the tractor. Willie had other ideas about his day, but Skip was unusually persistent and Willie finally agreed that the repair ought to be done. I worked alongside on a project of my own, pausing to photograph their work. Our discussion of the morning's work occurred a few months later.

WILLIE (looking at the stack of photos): "*That* looks like a Ford tractor."

DOUG: "I remember that Ford tractor being here eight years ago. It sat inside for . . ."

WILLIE: "It sat outside for five years. Inside two. I took that on a bill from Roger McLaughlin because I wanted a tractor. Hundred ninety-seven dollars."

DOUG: "Why did Roger give up on it?"

WILLIE: "Well, he took the starter over to BOCES [an agricultural/vocational high school]—one of the boys that worked for him part time went to BOCES. He took the starter over to rebuild it. Never got it back. Got kinda disgusted with it. That's how I got it. It sat in his barn for three months, right in the free stalls. It got all eat up with the acids from the cow manure—oh, that's bad on a machine. It was just like it had gone through a fire. That's why it rusted out."

DOUG: "You saw it as worth a lot of money fixed up?"

WILLIE: "At that time you could get them pretty reasonable. But you can't now. I figured that if I put wheels on it, got a starter for it, and got it running I could use it for woods work—which is what I'm doing.

"The wheels are off a big truck—twenty-two-inch. I had to cut the Ford wheels down to mount them on, to weld them in. And the front wheels are cut down to thirteen inches. I turned the cast iron hubs down to fit a thirteen-inch rim. The drawbar was missing; we built that out of parts. The throttle control was all rusted off, and the generator was missing. The radiator bottom was broke right off, so we took it off and rebuilt it. Soldered it back on. Gas tank was full of rust. Took that all off, cleaned it, blew it out. Cleaned all the manure out from in between the radiator and the hood—it was really full of manure. Changed the distributor over to where I had an exterior rather than an interior coil. Usually when it gets to be rainy weather they don't want to start with the other type of coil, and they burn out too easy. And I changed it over so that I'm using an eight-volt battery instead of a six. Starts in the wintertime now just like it does in the summer. The other day Ray Dean didn't think it would start—it was zero—but it started right up. Usually they say a Ford tractor won't start up after the first frost in the fall.

48 Lighting up the Rosebud.

"We had to put a bumper on the tractor because Skip was using it too rough in the woods [laughs]. We were using it to get wood out, and he was driving over little trees and everything with no bumper and no grille—he was going to spoil the radiator!"

"We're getting ready to cut the parts for the grille. Skip got the metal and stuff ready and hunted up some of the pieces to use. I'm lighting up the torch. . . . They had the old mailbox out there—that old overgrown mailbox—and they were cleaning that down to paint it. Julie and Sheila [Willie's daughters, but only Sheila is in the photograph]. Sheila looks a little sour, but it's more or less that she's watching what I'm doing. She's got full interest in what's going on . . . and Christopher's [Willie's grandson] looking at that flame. In fact, all those eyes are coming down to that flame. Mine too. I'm setting it, adjusting it. You're supposed to use a Rosebud torch for heating, but if you use a Rosebud on light metal it's just a waste of heat. I have a Rosebud, but I only use it on heavy metal. And there's the ring [a seventeen-inch circular piece of metal behind Willie, outside the shop; right side of photo, middle] that we used for the bumper—the arch . . . I don't understand, though—I've got the welding helmet on and I'm lighting the torch. . . . Oh, I remember, we were heating the arms that held the bumper and bending the arms together to weld the six-inch channel on. You can see it in the next photograph."

WILLIE: "This shows the detail of the arms that we built to hold the bumper. We put the arms on the axle, then bent them out straight [to be welded to the bumper]. There's more strength in it that way. It had to be bent around a little in order to fit the bolt hole on the axle and to miss the shroud in the grille [see also photo 55]. The original had a bracket that bolted on the same way. . . . Jeez, I'm set right up in safety features—I've even got my safety shoes and my safety gloves on for a change" (laughs). [49]

DOUG: "How did you come up with that design?"

WILLIE: "The original bumper is almost the same size as the one we're making, but they're a little different shape. The original has arms that come off the axles and onto a flat piece of metal. There is an arch built up there with fancy grillwork. It has bars so nothing can get to the grille. When I got the tractor the bumper was gone. The original grille was rusted and eat so bad it was beyond repair. [50]

"You could have fixed the old piece but you would have spent more time on it than it was worth. There's about three inches gone off the bottom—it was eat right into the crank hole, so bad it wouldn't hold a true form to work from. You would have had to do a lot of building back, adjusting, measuring—

49 Welding the new bumper
onto the tractor.

because there are little pins that come out of each top corner that sets up into the top of the hood to hold it in place—they'd have to line up just right for it to work."

DOUG: "I always wonder what you see through that helmet when you're welding. Can you see the details pretty well?"

WILLIE: "Perfect. I wear the lens that lets you see all your melting metal and everything. If you can't see what's melting, what's blending together—that is where a lot of people run into problems. They don't blend their metals together—they don't flow 'em. And that's why a weld doesn't hold. You've got to be able to see that flow of metal. You've *got* to be able to see it. There are different lenses for the helmets—they go by number, a code that tells how dark it will be. I use one of the darkest ones they've got. If you get too light a lens you can't see the full flow of your metal—it's just like not wearing any at all when you're braising. You can't see what you're doing—you can't study it. The glow is too bright—it's like looking at the sun, almost . . . but you know, you can photograph more than you can see. In fact, sometimes I think the photograph shows more than *I* see."

DOUG: "When I look at these photographs I see you close down, studying."

WILLIE: "You've got to be. If you don't see your metals and know how they're flowing you haven't got a weld. You get what I told you before—bubblegum weld—if you don't flow it. It just bubbles on and it doesn't penetrate to hold your metals together . . . you've seen bubbles in the metal on some welds—well, that's what they call a bubblegum weld."

"Skip used a piece from an old gas furnace for the radiator cover. There was a perforated screen on the front of it—pretty heavy, about a thirty-secondth.

"You see—we thought about putting another piece of channel on it, welded right onto the piece we put on there. But if we'd done that we'd cut down a lot of wind—air to keep the radiator cool. If you cover the radiator too much with metal when the tractor's working hard it'll overheat. So we came up with the idea of putting the arch over it—that's when we came up with the ring. [52, 53]

"The ring was off an old stack flue—you can see it laying in the background in the first photograph."

DOUG: "Stack flue?"

WILLIE: "Smokestack from Brasher Iron Works. A fella picked it up at Clotman's, a junk dealer up in Massena. He was going to make a furnace out of it, but he got discouraged in the middle of the job and bought one instead. He gave it to me and I made a furnace out of it, but I had to cut some pieces off of it. That was one of the pieces I cut off—it was seventeen inches in diameter.

50 The original grille, rusted away at the bottom.

51 Considering the part from the gas furnace to be made into a radiator cover. Here the piece is put into place and marked.

That's the furnace in the back of the shop—at least part of it. I had to cut more off when I put the hot water unit on the top. It's heavy, a quarter-inch, regular old smokestack.

"We cut the ring to size. . . . We held it up to see how high we wanted it, and then we straightened the edges so it set straight down on the bumper. I see you've still got the mailbox in that one. Julie and Sheila were working on that— I think Christopher was up working on it too." [53]

DOUG (to Julie, who is gazing over Willie's shoulder): "What were you doing, painting it?"

JULIE (emphatically): "No, sanding it! Sanding it down to get it ready to paint."

DOUG: "Did you paint it?"

JULIE: "Not yet. It still needs to be sanded—a lot. It needs the insides done, too. I want to paint it blue, but Willie says we'll paint it the color of the one that's there—black."

WILLIE: "We used the same screws that were holding it in the furnace to put it on the tractor—regular sheet metal screws. It made a pretty nice job—

52, 53 Willie cuts an arch
from the metal ring.

the brush doesn't get into it. But if you're out in the field where there's a lot of seeds or anything like that, you've got to be careful and keep it clean. It's not that seeds go through it, but little leaves and stuff will stick to it, shut off the air, and make your tractor overheat. But you've got the same thing happening if you don't have a cover on the radiator—stuff goes into your radiator—plugs it up—makes the engine overheat." [54]

DOUG: "I was surprised at how heavy a piece of metal it was. Looking at it beforehand it didn't look heavy enough to do the job."

WILLIE: "But once you get it mounted on there—the way you mount it—it strengthens it—strengthens it an awful lot."

DOUG: "Where did that piece of metal come from?"

WILLIE: "That was taken out of . . . let's see . . . that was in the water-works in Waddington. They put a new heating system in. It had all burned out and was putting gas fumes right out into the building. The guy who took it out just brought it out here and dropped it off. They had to get rid of it anyway, so . . . it was supposed to go to the dump, but he just brought it out here and dumped it off. I'm still kicking around quite a bit of it up there—falling over it once in a while . . . that's why the place looks so junky—I never throw any-thing away. But on the other hand, you can always find something to use."

DOUG: "If you look in the beginning photographs it sits there in the cor-ner—not intended to be used for the tractor at that point."

WILLIE: "At that point, no—that was just sitting outside. Skip started walk-ing around looking, and that's what he came up with. We needed something to put on for the grille."

DOUG: "I remember so many times at the shop—you'll start walking around looking for a part or a piece to make a part, and you'll walk around for quite a while until you come to something that's right for the job. It's interesting watch-ing you because I can't anticipate what you'll come up with."

"I'm cutting off the excess from the bottom. We made it curve around the bot-tom to protect the radiator from the low stuff." [55]

WILLIE: "We finished with putting the strips on the sides." [56]

DOUG: "Do you remember why?"

WILLIE: "It would be a lot safer that way."

DOUG: "Skip cut his hand on it, remember?"

WILLIE: "Right . . . in fact he's the one who's doing the drilling—putting it on there. Oh, those edges are sharp! Those edges we are putting on there origi-nally came out of the furnace—they held that piece in the furnace. (Willie shuffles through the photographs to find one that shows the furnace in the back-

54 Willie and Skip attach the radiator cover they have just cut to size.

55 Cutting off the excess
from the bottom of the grille.

56 Skip attaches protective
strips to cover the sharp
edges of the radiator cover.

57 Willie trims the arch to match the width of the bumper.

ground.) See, there were little furring strips around it. We took those and cut them and put them in there. That was the air intake in the furnace."

DOUG: "I wondered if the metal on the tractor was good enough to screw into."

WILLIE: "You don't see it, but it's double thickness in front. There's a heavy plate under the skin. The thin metal goes over it to give it form, but there's a heavy plate underneath. The original grille was held into the heavy plate—not onto the thin metal that forms the looks of it. So we were drilling through both pieces."

DOUG: "It seems like the two of you work well together."

WILLIE: "He's worked with me long enough to know just how to go ahead and work with me."

DOUG: "In these photographs you're more or less taking turns. He's begun this part of the project and you've stepped aside. I remember him cutting his finger pretty badly—then he went out there and got those pieces off that radiator. He just took the tools and took over for a while. Here you're helping him hold it in place."

"We finished up with that half-round. Eventually I want to put bars up and down in there, to keep something from going back through it. I'm trimming it off the same thickness all around, more or less for looks. It was all rough—the way they cut it at the junkyard. I wanted to straighten it out; make it better than it was. So when I put the bars in I'll make them the same width, and they'll fit any place I put them. [57]

"Now I've got a tractor to use in the woods. If you hit small trees or something like that, the bars will help support the arch. I've used it a lot since it's been on there—an awful lot, for moving cars out and in. It's just exactly the height of a car bumper. It's better than the original—you couldn't push a car with the original because it had a hitch on the front. I'll put a hitch back on, but I'll make it so I can snap it on and off. And the fact that it's solid all the way up there makes it work beautifully for pushing wagons or anything—it's high enough to even catch the rack of a wagon."

From odds and ends of parts and materials a machine regains its usefulness. The rebuilding of the front of the tractor shows specific ways such parts and pieces are put to use. This example also shows some of the engineering skill needed for even a relatively simple job. The acquisition and rebuilding of the machine show how an informal economy develops because bricoleurs like Willie have a use for what others throw away.

Land, House, and Bridge

The concept of bricolage can also be applied to the way Willie lives on the land. Building a bridge or a house, however, is part of Willie's personal history. In this sense one's biography can be thought of as "bricolage"—unlikely elements influenced by what is finally a mysterious mixture of improvisation, opportunity, and accident.

Willie moved to the North Country from Washington, D.C., in the early 1950s. In Washington he had been a mechanic and body man. He tells stories about how Harry Truman used to sneak out of the White House through a basement elevator to go drinking with him and his friends from the garage. I don't exactly believe him, but I don't actually disbelieve him either.

Willie met a young woman in Washington who was working in the city and living with her brother. Pauline and Willie married and moved to her hometown in the northeastern corner of New York State. Willie worked as a mechanic and body man for a number of garages, gradually moving to Massena, a hundred miles from Pauline's hometown, as the Seaway project was getting under way. At the time Willie signed on the Seaway project he had been out of work for three months from "too much paint in my lungs." The Seaway job provided an opportunity to get back to work outside a body shop. Willie recalls:

"I wasn't supposed to go back to work yet, but I figured that if I was working outside it would help. That's when I went to work on the Seaway. I went up to the Union Hall one day and went to work the next. Mechanic-welder. I worked as a mechanic and did any welding that needed to be done. From what I understood I was the only one on the Seaway job that had a mechanic-welding book. That's the biggest book you can get. [The "book" is the union classification record.]

"I fixed equipment—not that different from what I'm doing now. I worked as a Cat mechanic for two seasons out there. I did motor jobs, transmission jobs, things like that."

An industrial accident changed Willie's life. He remembers:

"We were taking a 250-foot boom apart, one they were using with the drag lines for dredging the Eisenhower lock channel. They were taking the boom apart, putting it on flatcars, and shipping it to Oregon for a job there.

"One of the joint plates dropped on me, about fifteen feet before it hit me on the head. It weighed about 140, 150 pounds. They called it 150. That never knocked me out, either, but I've got a spot in my hard hat I hammered back out! There's a spot on my head where the Doc pulled the crushed skin off and pulled the other skin over it. It's funny, all of the pictures you've got—they don't show any of that scar up there, where my hair is thin."

Willie did not take medical disability for the accident, although maladies related to the injury have continued to affect his health. He gradually went into work for himself and bought the land he now lives on:

"When I first met Ralph, I was in a wheelchair from the accident on the Seaway and he was just out of the hospital. Neither of us were ever supposed to work again. Ralph had strained the muscles of his heart; they told him he didn't have but a few months, maybe a year or two at the most. He was sitting around his farm and I was sitting around my trailer going crazy with nothing to do. He'd come and pick me up in the morning—I didn't even have a car in those days—and take me to the farm. Some machinery broke down—there was an old welder sitting there—I fired her up and used it! I put things back together, or made trailers and things. Next thing I knew they had half the farmers coming in for me to do work. I didn't take the job—I got *pushed* into it. Ralph and Sonny were telling everyone else about it and they were coming in to get work done. I started going up and driving tractor for them—they got the crops in and off on time for a change! We both worked at it slow like; that was the one and only time in my life I ever had a tan!

"It got so that me and Ralph were running the farm. One day he says, 'You like the woods?' 'What do you mean? Walking in the woods, working in the woods, or just being in the woods?' I says. 'Any one,' he says. 'The answer is yes,' I says; 'it don't matter which.'

"So we started in his woods, fifteen acres he had on the end of his south field. We went in the late fall because it was swampy and it had to freeze. You wouldn't believe the guff I took on that—'You're going to kill him, you're going to put him into the grave!'—everyone except his wife—she understood. We started up kind of slow, but after a while there wasn't a man that could keep up with either of us. Ralph always said he'd never live to see that forest grow back, and he couldn't believe it when I took him back there in the spring—you remember—I showed you! There where the second growth is coming on strong—the samples and oaks—just little trees when Ralph and I were cutting there in the fifties. Now those are beautiful trees."

58 The road to Willie's woodlot.

"We cut pulp logs and then we cut elm and basswood that was made into the cheeseboxes at the old cheese factory. They would cut veneer off elm and basswood and make those circular cheeseboxes. Now and then we could sell logs to the hardwood mill in Potsdam. I remember once I dropped a big oak. I told Ralph, 'You take that log to the mill.' He must have forgotten about it, because I found that log out in the woods a few weeks later. When I asked him he said they weren't taking oak at the mill, they already had plenty of oak. He thought it was white oak. I told him to take it anyway. We brought those logs in there and the man at the mill says, 'We don't need no more oak,' but then he looks closer and he says, '*This* oak is different! Bring all you got of this oak!' See, it was red oak. You could see on the trunk, at the base of the log. That is the stuff they make flooring out of. We got seventy or eighty dollars out of that one tree, and that was twenty years ago. Every time we'd get a check from the pulp company or the hardwood mill—we'd take half of it to pay on the land. We paid six hundred dollars for the twenty-three acres I've got here. Ralph and I bought it on shares, and then I bought him out."

WILLIE: "This is back in Bill Murphy's woods, parts off a bobsled that Ralph and I used when we were logging. We used it for nine years, then somehow or other we lost track of it and it rotted apart. But in the meantime, when this one was left set, we used a sled behind our dozer. That had eight-foot runners on it—it was just a sled, there was no bob to it. I've still got the steel for those, which I was figuring to build back up and never have. We used that on our dozer—and I put an eleven-foot bed on that, and that was what we hauled our pulp with behind the dozer.

"When the weather wasn't too bad we'd use the horse on the sled. She'd move it right off—we had a mare—oh, she was a nice horse. When we were logging we'd hitch her up, and she'd find her way out easier than you could lead her out. Oh yes! She'd go out in the field, and one of the Murphy boys was usually out there, and they'd unhitch her and turn her around and she'd come right back in the woods. She'd come right back to where we were, and we'd hitch her up and back out she'd go. Skidded a lot of logs that way with her. This wagon that sits out in the yard—I made that up and had a set of fills on it. We used her in that for summer work. The fill bars that go up to hook on her harness for steering. I had a set of those on this wagon out here. We hauled an awful lot of pulp out in that."

DOUG: "Bill asked me to take this photo of the bobsled parts—it obviously meant a lot to him." [95]

WILLIE: "Oh yeah, because that was his grandpa's [Ralph]. Me and his grandpa got it out and used it. He used to ride it out and in. He'd hitch his sled behind it and ride in behind it. Him and Leonard and Mike. On weekends, when they didn't have school and we'd go back to work, they'd take their hand sled and tie behind it and ride it in. Oh, they used to have a ball doing that!"

DOUG: "Why did you give up on the horse and start using the dozer?"

WILLIE: "She was getting pretty well up in years."

DOUG: "I suppose it was slow—one log at a time."

WILLIE: "Hey, she'd take a good-sized log and go! She'd stop and wind herself and then take off again by herself—you didn't have to be with her. Just tie the lines up on her hang strap, on her hames, and let her go. She'd wind herself about three or four times on the way up because we had some good-sized logs. It was the first time it had been logged in quite a while. We cut out the old sugarbush that had grown itself out. Plus there was a lot of elm we took out, too.

"Ralph and I bought this piece of land with the idea that we were going to log it. When we bought it that's all we were going to do with it. I was living down on the Norfolk–Madrid Road. It got to be a hassle to drive back and forth all the time, so I moved my little trailer right out here. Hooked up lights and things. We lived there quite a while with no lights. We used the gas lantern, and the trailer was the size that the gas lantern would heat it until it got cold weather. And then we had a little stove that used about five gallons a week to heat it [laughs]. Couldn't do that anymore!

"Then when Ralph decided to get out from under it because of the tax—we paid fifty-fifty on the tax—we did that for four or five years, I guess—then he decided he wanted to sell out his share. So I bought him out for $125. . . . I'll never forget his face though, when I took him back and showed him in the woods the way I wanted to trim it out and things—how it was grew up. He says, 'I'll never live to see it.' And . . . I think it was eighteen years after we'd cut out the sugarbush—oh, we've got beautiful trees back there. I took him back—he got out of the Jeep and just looked around. About four years ago. . . . He says, 'I never thought I'd live to see it, but you told me I would.'

"We had a ball together. We put in a lot of hours working in the woods. Not only this woods; there's one behind this one—I don't know how many acres there are in that one, and then down towards Waddington we cut pine there for two or three winters. We cut pine pulp. That was all done with a dozer and a sled with an eleven-foot bed."

As Willie's health improved he went to work for a local Saab dealership while continuing to fix farmers' machines and tools. After the woodlot was logged it was left to grow for twenty years. In the meantime Willie built his large Quonset shop,

59 Bobsled parts at the edge of the woods.

which was heated by oil. When the price of oil increased fivefold in the early seventies, the woodlot became important as a source of fuel for the shop and the house that was eventually built. The woodlot lies across Brandy Brook from the lot where Willie lives. You get to the lot by traveling a mile and a half across a county bridge and Ralph's field. In the spring and fall, when the fields are wet, it is often impossible to cross them with a tractor. Even in the best woodcutting season—late fall before the snow piles heavily—it is often impossible to get to the woods across Ralph's fields.

Willie built a bridge years ago, but it was removed by the Conservation Department because it allegedly cut down the water flow. Over the years Willie made plans for another bridge that would be permanent but would not restrict the flow of the brook. Pieces were eventually gathered, and the bridge was constructed.

Willie comments, "I looked at that [64] and it looked like Niagara Falls at first! It makes it look funny with all the water stretched all the way into the woods. What looks funnier yet is that ice coming down towards it. It's broke away behind it.

"The concrete tiles were put in there by hand and come-alongs. They were pulled into place with come-alongs and cables. As you look at the bridge on the far side there's a big tree stump. It shows on 62. I hooked the come-alongs onto that to pull them across. I pushed them down in the creek with a tractor. Dick Green and I. I just lined them up by eye and built the frame on top of it.

"The frame is made out of some junk steel that was thrown away, and I took the pieces and welded them together to make what I wanted."

"I remember somebody dropping that stuff off," I say.

"Yeah, they were short pieces—twelve-foot pieces I welded right above the center beam.

"You can see some of the rock we used. We picked a lot of the rock out of the creek bed. In 62 you can see the red-rod in there before I put the stones at each end of it, to hold it down into place."

"I remember soon after that, around Halloween, Sue [my wife] had just come back from a trip; I came over here and Skip, you, and I brought a lot of loads of rock over."

Willie answers, "We went up on Dean Streeter's place, to his pasture, and got them. See, where these planks are laying here [62—the planks that are laid from the ground to the bridge]—there is an awful depth below those planks where that is filled in with all stones, about twenty-five ton of stones. That's twenty-five ton on each end of the bridge. All by hand.

60 Willie has moved the concrete tiles into place and put
the iron rails, which will be
the main bridge supports, on
them. The portable welder is
in the foreground, with a
cardboard box covering the
motor (August).

61 Willie has finished the bridge superstructure and bolted on the ash planks. Colter and Willie are looking for frogs (September).

62 We have fastened the bridge to the trees on the bank with reinforcing rods. Willie will fill the space between the end of the bridge and the bank with rocks and cement (late September).

63 Bridge completed (December).

64 The bridge is tested by spring floods (March, two years later).

"I cut the ash for the planks from my woodlot and took them up to Dean Streeter. He cut the lumber up for me. I trimmed up the edge after I put on the top plank."

"Did you ever get around to cutting those bolts off [61] that are sticking up through the planks?"

"No, I never did get those cut off." Willie pauses. "I kind of wanted to ease off on cutting them off because I was thinking about putting up a railing of some type, a little higher than that. See, the girls drive the garden tractor over there, and now they drive the Ford tractor. A little railing would help—a skid rail of some sort would be better than that plank laying there now. I was thinking about putting something like that on it. It wouldn't hold back that much water. I think I'd take something round—like a black ash or hickory would be the best. So if a wheel came up against it, it'd just rub. I'd only use a four- or five-inch diameter. It wouldn't make that much difference. But it would be a safety factor in crossing the bridge. I'll probably be taking the car over in there because of the trailer sitting in there. I'm going to have a road all the way over, anyway. And when those planks are wet they're a little slippery.

"The re-rod is important in holding the whole bridge in place. The re-rod is welded to the I-beams of the bridge, and it runs over and is hooked to the tree. Afterwards I pushed it down lower and when I laid my header wall, like you see here [61]—when I laid the header wall I laid it over the re-rod. The header wall helps hold the re-rod down. The big problem is not having it wash away in the spring. Plus I put cement down on the stones to help seal it. I had a lot of bags of cement that were no good—they were hard—but they worked down there! They cemented a lot of that rock together. I put the bags on top of the rocks and then took the big sledge and busted them up. When the rains came it made it into cement."

"My eye doesn't go to that—the re-rod—and yet it's an important element."

"That's three-quarter re-rod, and you've got a lot of strength there," Willie says. "And that's low for high water. High water is usually a foot, foot and a half over the bridge. It comes right up to the back of the house here. And the bridge has not moved at all, not one bit. I check every spring. And it hasn't washed a bit, the header walls are holding. But every spring you've got to go down—like you see all that brush and stuff—you've got to go down and clean all that out. Beaver cut the stuff and it floats down and sticks. So every spring you clean that out."

"Would the Conservation Department come down and give you any grief about this?" I ask.

"One Conservation man looked at it and said 'No problem.' See, you can't restrict the stream over 5 percent, I think they said. And I haven't got 2½ percent. He figures I've got maybe 1 percent restriction. See, they thought I was going to put a big abutment in the middle and everything. But instead of using an abutment I used a tile, and you've got water flow through it, and you've got a strong system. It's strong enough to hold a load—well, I've had a dozer across it and it never even shook. I guess that's around six or seven tons. Or if you load up a load of wood, you've got quite a bit of weight there. My lowboy there, when that's loaded you can put a cord and a half of pulpwood onto it and that gets you right up to six or seven ton."

"This has made a lot of difference, obviously, in being able to get your wood out. I think back to the difficulties you had four or five years ago . . ."

"Yeah, every time the field gets too much snow in it you can't get through it, or so much mud in it you can't get through it. You don't want to cut up the guy's field circling around every time. This has made an awful difference."

"I remember years ago," I say, "I was over at the shop one day and somebody came by and said those tiles were available—they were left over from some job or something?"

"They put in all new on Highway 345 and that was some they had taken out and put in new. They went from the big cement tile, because they held so much frost, they went from that big cement tile down to the corrugated steel. They were there for the taking. If someone didn't take them they had to haul them back to the barns. Meryl Sharp got some of them, and I got what was left. We took my lowboy and we used it on the back of Tommy Lawrence's Allis-Chalmers with the front-end loader on it. As I remember I had to fix the front-end loader to do it."

"At the time you were talking about building a bridge, and I didn't think it was ever going to happen."

"A lot of people didn't think it was going to happen," Willie answers.

"I don't mean to sound cynical about it, but you have a lot of projects going on, and this was before you built your house."

Willie laughs: "Those concrete tiles laid there for quite a while before I got to them!

"This bridge is stronger than the bridge they've got down here that the traffic uses. There's not much that can give out on it. The I-beams came out of a bridge somewhere. I don't know where they came from. They were in a bunch of junk and I got it. A guy hauled it in for me. They were in a scrap pile. They actually came out of a bridge somewhere. But they did the road over and they had to take out the bridge that was in. They did the new bridge altogether different, so they couldn't use any of that. Plus, when they took these out, they cut them. That's why I had to weld it all back together. That metal laid up at the shop for about two and a half years. It came in one fall. It laid through all the snow and everything. Then part of it laid down here, out here in the yard. That's what I got hollered at about: 'You going to use that stuff? If you don't I'm going to get rid of it!'"

Willie built his house the same way he fixes machines or constructs a bridge. Although he bought some of the material, he accumulated a lot of it through barter and salvage.

The typical way of buying a house in America, of course, is to amass a down payment (either saved above the cost of rent or perhaps lent or given by a relative), arrange a mortgage, and enter into a long-term—usually twenty- to thirty-year—financial arrangement based on steady payments. At this time the average new house in the United States costs just over a hundred thousand dollars.

For several reasons, Willie did not obtain his house in the typical way. To begin with, there is the simple fact of economy. The wages of a workman in Willie's bracket supply immediate family needs but do not provide savings for expenses such as a down payment on a house. Willie first housed his family in a small trailer, then a larger one, which were still sizable investments.

But beyond the pure economics of the situation, when you are capable of making your way through the material world, even if the important ingredient of time is in short supply, it is simply reasonable to think in terms of doing things for yourself. Put simply, Willie built his own house because he knows how to. And more important, given the financial constraints, he built his house because he was able to accumulate the materials largely through trade, favors paid back, and barter. The house became a possibility because it was made through the same bricolage by which Willie makes the other machines in his life.

A house can be built this way only in a community without strict regulation, for Willie's house is an improvised design whose elements exist in the gray netherworld beyond the strict confines of a zoning code.

When I first met Willie he lived with his family in a house trailer half a mile below his shop, on a two-acre lot directly across the creek from his twenty-three-acre woodlot. Willie talked a great deal about building a house during these years, but my impression was that his time was used up with work for customers, unpaid work for friends, and the work required by his own tractors, cars, Rototillers, snowmobiles, and chain saws, and by recurrent medical problems from his industrial accident. It seemed unlikely there would ever be time for a project of such magnitude as building a house.

The house, however, was built (and is still in the process of being built, for several projects are ongoing) in the way most of Willie's projects are completed. Willie and his son dug the basement with a neighboring farmer's bulldozer. A block mason put up the cellar walls to pay back a favor. Willie said simply, "He's a friend of mine." Most of the lumber was cut from his woods. There was a lot of standing ash, so Willie had it sawed into two-by-fours for studding even though it is a much harder wood than is generally used for framing. This meant that holes had to be drilled for nails, since it is nearly impossible to drive a nail into green ash. The sheeting for the house was made from basswood. This was also an unusual choice, but Willie decided that even though it is not high-quality wood it would work well where covering rather than strength was needed. Besides, he had a lot of it.

Another farmer who depends regularly on Willie to maintain his equipment offered him several standing hemlocks in exchange for a repair on his field sprayer. The hemlocks (a good substitute for pine) were huge trees deep in the forest. Willie's chain saws were too small to cut through the trees at the base, so we used my chain saw, which has a twenty-two-inch blade, but even with that the cuts had to be made from both sides. We worked for two cool days in an uncharacteristically dry September cutting the huge trees and dragging them out, one by one, with a small tractor. All the wood was sawed into lumber at a hundred-year-old sawmill run by a retired plant laborer fifteen miles to the northeast. Willie rebuilt the gasoline engine that powers the sawmill in exchange for the sawing.

Additional lumber came from a nearby barn that was torn down and traded as salvage. Siding for an attached woodshed came from a neighbor's house, salvaged when the neighbor stripped the house, insulated, and replaced the old siding with plastic. The outside back stairs were left over from building a fire escape for a neighbor who housed state mental-health patients. They came originally from a factory in a nearby town, salvaged by a junk dealer after the factory burned. The stairs were slightly twisted but were extraordinarily heavy and certainly serviceable. Willie had accumulated glass for the house over several years from discarded windows. He made his own insulated glass casings. The wiring and plumbing materials were picked up similarly through several trades, and people gave Willie used sinks or bathtubs just for getting them out of the way. The primary materials that were purchased were insulation, roofing, which was also used for the sloping sides of the house, interior paneling, and concrete blocks. Willie figures the house cost $4,000, "paid as I go." And while the final result is unlikely to find its way into the pages of *Fine Homebuilding*, it is indeed serviceable, reasonably warm and tight—a home. And it was built a day here, a day there, usually in time wrested from the shop, with customers still wanting Willie's attention to solve problems of their own.

As an ongoing project the house has fought with its environment. You can say it has adapted to the environment slowly, over time. There have been steps back as well as forward. During the first winter, water drained down the basement walls, froze, and heaved the new concrete so it cracked in several places. When the frost went out of the basement walls they settled back into place, and repairs were begun. Earth tremors (the North Country has the second most frequent occurrence of earthquakes in the United States) further unsettled the walls. Springs run under the house. Willie installed a drainage system, but it has not always been able to handle the flow from the springs. When they are blocked by freezing, the basement takes on water fast.

The house as envisioned will generate its own heat and electricity. The electrical system will run off a windmill of Willie's design. For years he has been saving car batteries that will be recharged by a wind-powered generator. His plans for the windmill use blades made from fifty-five-gallon drums with slots cut in them. Willie explains that the primary problem with propeller-driven windmills is that the bearings on the shaft can never take the uneven pressure of the wind on the propeller. As one blade goes behind the tower, for example, the wind is temporarily blocked, setting up a momentary shift in pressure on the other blade of the propeller. Willie's design utilizes blades that work almost like the impeller on a rotary engine, spinning with even pressure around a central shaft. The fifty-five-gallon drums are cheap and easy to find. Willie has assembled parts of the electrical system, and he relies on the local power company for electricity until the project is finished.

The house will use a combination of solar and wood heating. The solar heat system will be integrated into a greenhouse being built on the south side. Solar collectors will circulate hot water into a two-thousand-gallon tank to be situated underground at the front of the house. The tank, a gasoline storage tank Willie got for nothing, needs to have its small rust holes welded over, and it must be moved into the concrete-walled room Willie has built under his front porch. Several details remain to be worked out in the heating system, but progress has been steady if gradual. Willie built a beautiful fireplace in the basement, using round stones picked out of several rock piles. He designed air chambers in the fireplace, with a fan to circulate the warm air through the house. The fireplace also has a door that converts it into an efficient wood furnace. Even the sandstone mantel was gained through a deal with a neighbor. Though the basement is now cluttered with building projects connected with the house, Willie's vision is of a warm and comfortable space for relaxing and maybe a little "inventing."

The process goes on and on. The machines Willie uses to get from one place to another, to work in his woods or his garden—are all made from leftovers reenvisioned, redesigned for specific needs that are almost always different from their

65, 66 Willie's house, exterior and interior.

67–68 Willie's "doodle-bug"—made from a 1929 International truck rear axle and fifteen-speed transmission; an early 1930s Fordson tractor front axle and seat; a fifteen-horsepower, two-cylinder Wisconsin motor from a hay baler; front wheels cut down from fifteen-inch Chevrolet car rims; a steering box from a 1942 one-and-a-half-ton truck; and a gas tank from an old outboard motor. In super low the doodlebug will pull an enormous load; in high gear it will go forty miles an hour. Behind the doodle-bug in photo 68 is a trailer Willie has made to haul firewood.

original purpose. A Rototiller gains an engine from a snowmobile. Truck boxes are converted into trailers. A Saab enters its fourth hundred thousand miles with an amalgam of parts taken from Saabs of many years and models and even cars of other makes. As a machine wears out it is often redesigned and put to a different use. As the house settles and shifts it is changed to sit more securely on the land. In all these ways, through the odds and ends of the world, Willie makes his way. To understand the *nature* of work, it is necessary to see its organic connection to this purpose.

69, 70 Willie talks about his
1929 Model A Ford: "You
start, you do one part, and
when you get that done you
do another. So it's done in
sections. You don't try to do
an overall job at one time.
One thing at a time."

71 Willie breaks his homemade saw loose from the
frozen ground.

72 Fixing the belt that runs
the saw from the power take-
off on the Ford tractor.

73 Sawing wood. The blade remains stationary as the cradle holding the wood is moved into its path.

74 Willie plows snow with his Jeep.

DOUG: "This thing looks like a decrepit piece of junk, but it's been around here ever since I have."

WILLIE: "Oh, it's powerful . . . I was plowing the snow away from the back of the shop, where I've got the small door. That was after we had one of those big snowstorms. It was all drifted in; I was breaking it up."

DOUG: "This kind of machine seems to go on indefinitely."

WILLIE: "Well, no. I locked that into low range and unhooked the linkage so they [other people who borrow the Jeep] couldn't get it out of low range. Now it can't be used for high speeds. That's why I've still got it. They're not beating it up with high speed. See, low range is third gear with that; I don't believe you can move over twelve miles an hour with it now. Used to be when we'd have a snowstorm I'd plow the road, from Highway 345 to the shop, even down here to the house [about a mile]. I'd plow with this before the snowplows would get around, because they usually didn't get here until 3:00 or 3:30, something like that. So I'd open it up so my customers could get out and in. That's quite a plow. That's the original plow and everything that came on the Jeep. I've had it ten, eleven years, maybe longer."

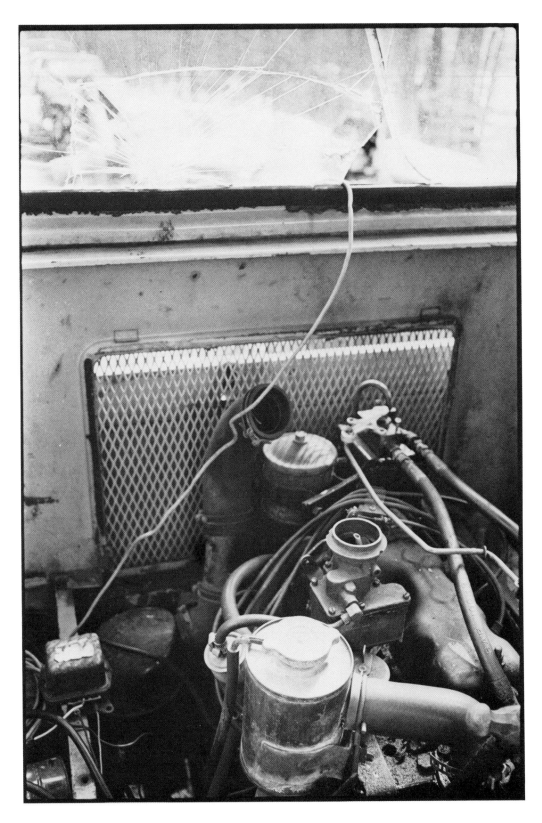

75 Jeep interior. There is no passenger seat or engine cover.

DOUG: "What's the wire coming through the hole in the window?"

WILLIE: "That runs back to the electric hoist on the boom on the back. That's twelve-volt electric. You've seen me pick up motors, even the front end of cars. There's no air cleaner on the carburetor, but I don't use it out where it's dusty. It does matter to a certain extent, but not that bad because I don't put it on the road and pick up a lot of dust, plus I keep the cowl off the motor. It uses the same air that I breathe setting in there, and it don't hurt me, so it shouldn't hurt it.

"That's not the original box you can see on photo 74. The original box lays down here all rusted and eat. This is a Chevrolet box—pickup box. I cut five and a half, maybe six inches out the middle of it and welded it back together so it would fit onto the Jeep frame. It was too wide for the Jeep without doing it. You don't have a photograph that shows where it was cut. I overlapped it there in the middle for extra strength. This also has a 250-pound ballast weight on the frame in the back so you can use it with the snowplow without raising the back end up. I put on the winch—that's for picking up a car and moving it.

"When I got it the motor was no good in it. I rebuilt the engine. And the transfer case was bad—I rebuilt that. That's when I locked it down into four-wheel drive at low range and I unhooked the handle so they couldn't be shifting around. Because if Lenny got into it he'd take right off down the road, forty-fifty miles an hour. And it'll move that fast. It's been up to Chazy [a hundred miles east]—I towed my Studebaker back from up at Chazy. Hooked right on to it and brought it back. I had it on the road for two years, I believe, then I put a snowplow license on it and had it on the road for about five years. It hasn't been too long since the plow license has run out. Now it's just a shop vehicle, but I use it in the woods too. I can get around in the woods with that where you can't with the tractor. You've got four wheels moving you there."

Indeed, the environment is managed by the hand of man.

Knowledge in the Body

There is a kinesthetic correctness to Willie's method. This in and of itself makes his mechanicking different from the work of the "parts changer," the formally trained by-the-book professional that I have referred to as the rationalized repairman. In the extreme case, the by-the-book mechanic works purely through the mind, taking direction from written instructions only rather than from the interplay of the theoretical and the empirical. But it is difficult to learn how hard to hit or twist a tool, or how to interpret the sounds of a running machine from written instructions. Often when you observe a mechanic who works only "by the book," you see that he is unable to use his body efficiently. Thus either materials are not pushed to their limits and the job gets stuck or they are pushed beyond their limits and parts are broken. Willie's working method builds on a detailed knowledge of materials and develops precisely the kind of tactile, empirical connection that leads to smoothly working rhythms, appropriate power and torque, and the interpretation of sounds and subtle physical sensations. Willie reads his body's messages and measures out the appropriate force of a blow or a twist; he will move things simultaneously, bang things harder than one would assume the material could take, then move gently, reading the pressure of the material. Robert Pirsig describes this quality of work:

There's what's called "mechanic's feel," which is very obvious to those who know what it is, but hard to describe to those who don't; and when you see someone working on a machine who doesn't have it, you tend to suffer with the machine.

The mechanic's feel comes from a deep inner kinesthetic feeling for the elasticity of materials. Some materials, like ceramics, have very little, so that when you thread a porcelain fitting you're very careful not to apply great pressures. Other materials, like steel, have tremendous elasticity, more than rubber, but in a range in which, unless you're working with large mechanical forces, the elasticity isn't apparent. (1974, 323)

I've chosen a number of conversations and jobs to show how this kinesthetic sense operates. The photographs isolate a moment in a work process, and they bring from Willie a description of what he ordinarily experiences. It is pushing words to expect that experience can be literally described, for the reality Willie experiences is taken for granted, a many-sided gestalt of theoretical, tactile, and auditory input.[13] It is difficult to put into words a complicated but utterly ordinary reality. Although I have chosen a number of examples to illustrate these ideas, all presentations of Willie's work in this book reflect to some degree the theme of the unity of work, the marriage of the hand and the mind, in solving practical problems.

"What I find hard about sharpening a chain saw, I say, is transferring the pressure from one hand to the other so you . . ."

". . . so you're keeping an even pressure going across—so you aren't rocking your file."

"I've watched you cut a slot in a log—it doesn't have to be in your vise—it doesn't have to be in a perfect situation—and no matter what position you're in

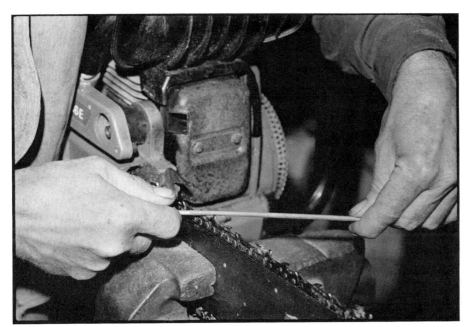

76, 77 "You've got to shift that pressure from one hand to another. As you go across the saw the pressure shifts on your file. If you hold it hard you can't feel the pressure. You're not gripping the file, you're more or less letting it float or glide right through."

you're still able to re-create the even pressure, the straight movement of the file across the teeth.

"It seems to me that painting cars is sort of like sharpening chain saws," I add. "From my vantage point it seems to be a question of keeping that movement steady."

"You've got to have the steady movement, the steady flow. And with your spray gun you're triggering it all the time to keep the air and paint flowing continuous. Each time you pull that trigger you spray. You've got to know when to hit that trigger and come back across and leave off . . . and come back again. Otherwise you've got a lot of flow in the paint you don't want."

"In the photo you see a little of the delicacy."

"Yeah—it looks like I'm holding the file real tender like. But you've got to shift that pressure from one hand to another—as you go across the saw the pressure shifts on your file. If you hold it hard you can't feel the pressure. You're not gripping the file, you're more or less letting it float or glide right through."

"I remember once when the Mad Russian was putting all his weight onto a nut he was trying to get loose. And you probably weigh half of what he weighs, I'd guess."

"Yup."

"You walked over and you broke it loose with a quick . . ."

". . . impact. Quick torque. Always better than a steady pull."

"It sticks in my mind—a quick move cracked it. And he'd been putting all his muscle into it."

"I remember that," Willie says. "Like Beswick, trying to get his tie-rod ends off. He was kind of hitting the wrong way. He was hitting more of a downward blow on it. I could tell from the battered part he was hitting. I used a hammer half as heavy as the one he had—one rap on each side—dropped it right out. He'd spent most of a day trying to get them out. He's good, but he didn't quite understand when I told him he had to hit toward the bottom of it with a kind of an upward swing. And your ball joints, they come out the same way. You've got to know just how to hit those or you'll bend them and you'll be out of alignment again. You've got to know which *way* to hit them. You've got to know how it feels. Raymond Dean—when he goes to tighten a bolt up he won't do it—he lets me do it. He'll twist them off. Oh, he's twisted off a lot of them!"

"So it doesn't necessarily come from experience."

"That's right. Some things you just don't pick up, some people. Where if you grow up with it you more or less have that knowledge built in. Some people can grow up with something and it don't—I don't know, there's just something that don't click right about it. They're not that interested in it. If they were interested in it they'd learn it. If you're not interested in something you might as well not get started."

One would expect to find physical finesse in tasks like sharpening chain saws, spraying paint, and pounding or twisting bolts. Willie's "hand knowledge" plays a significant role in the jobs I've used to illustrate his knowledge of materials. The hand knowledge, however, also is important in repairs that one would expect to require the least improvised procedures of any of Willie's work. This is seen in the following passage in which Willie disassembles a Saab transmission.

Unlike internal combustion engines, for example, transmissions are purely mechanical. They are, simply put, gears that transfer different degrees of power from the engine to the wheels of the car. Transmissions are complex because of the number of parts they contain and the way they are fitted together, yet the principle is straightforward and logical. Despite the straightforwardness, or pure mechanicalness, of transmissions, few mechanics repair them. This is in part because the ability to read a shop manual and understand the photographs that accompany the instructions is only part of the knowledge required to do the repair. Even in this most "objective" of procedures it is the subtle play of force and pressure, the simultaneous movement of parts, and an evaluation of wear through the sensations of the fingertips that guide and control the process of the work.

There are only brief legends for the photographs that follow because I intend to convey an impressionistic rather than a literal sense of the job at hand. The specific details of the disassembly are not relevant to the overall point of the discussion, which is the *un*conventionality of the hand skills involved in the job.

"I'm interested by the idea that this kind of work is complicated in a different way than other kinds of work you do," I begin. "If you look at the photographs of it, you can see step by step what's happening—it looks pretty simple here. But when you're actually involved in doing it, it seems extremely complicated. It seems complicated in a different way than, say, taking a bend out of metal."

Willie replies, "Even taking the cluster gear out of the body of this—which is showed in photo 86—when you take that out you've got to move these gears on the shaft, otherwise the housing catches it and you get into a bind. You can't take it out. These gears have got to slide on the shaft or they don't come out right. There's a bevel inside of the casing where the speedometer gear comes down in—it's made right inside the casing, and the one gear on the end here has got to slide off the shaft so that you can take the shaft out. And sometimes they're on there pretty solid. You'd be surprised.

78–87 Repairing a transmission.

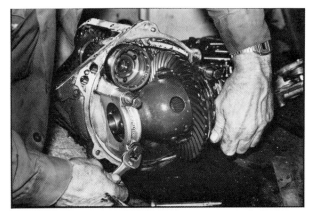

78–80 Removing the ring gear.

81–83 Saving a gasket.   84–86 Getting inside the transmission.

"When you reassemble it, it takes longer. You've got shim washers at the end of the shafts to make sure your bearings are seated right. Then your pinion shaft has a shim to make sure it sits out in the right position to hit the ring gear. It's a little more technical when you go putting them back together than it is taking them apart. Those gears have to all match up and run true. I do it by feel.

"If you take the gaskets off that way [81, 82, 83] it saves you a lot of scraping—and that is aluminum and you don't want to scrape aluminum any more than you have to. If you take your time taking it off it usually peels up because of the glue they use on it. It's possible to reuse it again if you use the silicon sealer, which I use quite often—saves the customer a lot that way, too.

"They say you never use a hammer when you work on a transmission, but this is one type of a transmission where they tell you to use a hammer, even in the book, in the manual. You've got to use a brass, or an aluminum drift. Like you see in photo 87. It's aluminum, so it won't batter the threads or anything on the shafts. But you don't bang on this the way you bang on other things. These aluminum housings—you can break them very easy—the mechanic Brad had working for him broke three of these transmission casings in a row. He didn't take his parts out in sequence the way the book told him to. I'd never seen one before, but I understand the engineering of the transmission. They are all basically the same, but some of them are a little more compact than others. The ones that are more compact are trickier than others. Did I tell you about the Datsun transmission I took apart last week? I had no idea how that was supposed to come apart. A guy had sheared a shifting pin in it. I took it apart and put it back together. And it worked. He went right back to speed shifting it, though!"

"How do you know when things need to be replaced when you're fixing them?" I ask. "How do you measure the tolerances? I remember they were going to replace all the bearings when they worked on my Sonnet transmission in Boston—they wouldn't check each one to see which ones were bad."

"Well, you check them for wear, and very seldom the Saab—the 95, 96, or even the Sonnet transmission, which is really the same—it's very seldom that you'll wear the gears so that you have to replace them. It's usually the bearings that give you the trouble. And if you catch them when the bearings start giving you the noise, you've got the same thing as a new transmission. You take them right out and check them. Check the races [the beveled rings into which the bearings turn]. You can see if they're rough; they usually shine like a mirror. If you've got a rough spot in them you can see it. Or if you can't see it you can feel it with the tip of your finger. One little rough spot will give you a licking in

87 Removing a shaft.

the transmission. But there's no reason to replace the ones that aren't worn.

"Even on this ring gear you've got shim spacers that go on each end. That's one right there [83]. They're different sizes—by the thousandths—to set your ring gear and pinion. If you get them too far apart it'll give you a whiny noise; you get them too close together and you'll run them out."

"How do you know what's just right?"

"I do it by feel, but you can get the regular Plastagauge—that's a small plastic gauge with different thicknesses of wire—to run through the gear that lets you know just what the thousandths are. I've done it by feel about all my life, I guess. My father was pretty good at it; I tried my hand at it too.

"The tolerances are real close. Now they've got different gear ratios on these transmissions, and you can't take one gear from the other and put it in another transmission that has a different gear ratio. Yet they're both four-speed transmissions. The gears won't match. There is a difference in the pitch of the teeth of them. Especially these teeth like you see in photo 86. But here again, if you didn't feel those tolerances when you were putting it back together you might try to force it."

Willie says with slow emphasis, "This is one transmission I love to work on."

"Why is that?"

"I don't know why—whether it's the engineering in it or what—I love to work on it. It's like a music box! The Saab 99 transmission isn't as hard to work on as this. You have to work at it from the end—you've got to work inside the casing. You don't see all the work you're doing. It's by feel. You know how it goes before you slide it in there, but you've got to make sure it's in the right position. You've got to translate your feelings—it's just like your fingers got eyes. If you've got a nut, or a stud, someplace and you want to know what size it is and you couldn't see it, you've got to be able to reach in, feel it, and tell. Those funny angles come in, too, when you're reaching up under the windshield, or under the dash.

"Like I say . . . it's the only transmission I've ever seen where you've got to use the hammer—they *tell* you to use the hammer. They tell you where to hit, and what to hit it with, and everything."

"But not everybody can follow the book. You told me Brad's first mechanic broke three transmission housings."

"The transmission book time was seven and a half hours—after it was on the table. I think I did it in four and a half hours—something like that. Kind of surprised him. But no one bothered me. I told him, just show me where the parts are I've got to have. Don't anyone bother me, I said, I just want the book and the parts. That's what he did—he laid the book right up there, and I went and worked at it. If no one bothers you it goes just like clockwork.

"To do this you've got to put yourself in the place of the engineer who built it in the first place. You've got to have the mechanical knowledge of engineering. But every job I do goes back into *my* computer. You've got to be able to remember from one job to the other how to make a job easier. You've got to take information from one job and apply it to the next. Like the Datsun transmission had a tail stalk on it—because it was a rear-wheel drive. It was one of those sports jobs. You had to take certain parts off the front of it before you could get the back off it. And when you put it back together you had to do it the same way. Just reverse yourself on it. I never got into one of those before. I had to figure it out myself. I just took the cap off it and looked it over to see what had to come out to get at what I wanted. There was a shifting fork I had to get to because he had sheared pins. He had the pin sheared off in low, second, and almost third and fourth. The little drive pin they use into them so they don't slide on the shifting shaft."

"How did you learn this? Did you get into trouble with transmissions you couldn't get out of when you were learning?"

"I grew up with it. The first transmission I ever did—let's see—that was a Model T—'25, or '26 Model T. The second one I did was a Model T. That was in a truck. Same problems as these—bearings go bad; gears go bad. They were a simple transmission to work on. Then I got into General Motors and had a Star. Had a Whippet—Overland Whippet they called it—'29. And the Model A's were more or less my pride and joy. That's why there's a '29 model A up in the garage.

"As the cars and the transmissions get more complicated you just stay with it. The only transmission I never got into—I started to get into them when they first came out—was the automatics. To do it right you've got to have the test block where you can set it up and put it under power to see what it is going to do. Where it is going to shift. They have what they call the fluid drive unit that powers—you can more or less tell what a transmission is going to do when you put it into power. The old Chevrolets—when they came out—that was back in . . . '48, '49—I think it was '49—they had vacuum shifts on them. When they first came out I was down in Washington, D.C., working on the automatics in taxicabs. None of the garages were set up for them at that time. So you more or less had to make it up as you went. I would set the bands, or the clutches. Dodge had a fluid drive shift—you just shifted it one time. Your general mechanic could take on new things like this. Now they go to school for it, and they only learn what they're taught. The problems aren't all in the manual."

Earlier I stated that the computer-directed "troubleshooting" and repair of increasingly computer-run automobiles represent the latest stage in the evolution of technique and the rationalization of repair. For many reasons this change in technology, I suggested, is accompanied by a change in the consciousness of the repairman. Seeing Willie's working method in this new technological context shows what happens to an earlier mind/body as the familiar working ground changes. But first it is necessary to describe what the computer does in an automobile.

This adaptation of computers to automobiles is not surprising, for the computer is, at least theoretically, ideally suited both to run and to help repair an automobile. In a modern car the ignition system—which regulates the intensity and the timing of the explosion in each cylinder, hundreds of times a minute—and the injection system—which mixes gasoline with air and injects it into the cylinders at precisely the appropriate moment to be ignited by the ignition system—are now typically directed and coordinated by computers built into the car. To bring the car "in tune" is to synchronize several mechanical and natural elements. Although the point gaps in an ignition system or the air/fuel mixture in an injection system can be set by a mechanic in a fairly straightforward manner, the natural elements in the system, such as air pressure, humidity, and temperature, are ever-changing. The computer is able to read as many elements of the environment or the automotive performance as there are sensors installed to monitor; the optimal balancing of these factors—tuning the car—is ultimately an objective determination most easily made, in an ideal situation, with a computer. The automobile can be programmed to tune itself continuously and to signal other computers when a particular component falls beneath a predetermined preformance level and should be replaced.

While this system has beautiful theoretical elegance, in practice it is, like all machines, prone to "irrational" behaviors—behaviors that cannot be accounted for by reading the objective information supplied to and from the computer. It might be that one of the variables has been left out or that a monitoring system has malfunctioned. It might be that not all the interrelationships within components have been figured into the compilations of the computer. In these circumstances the mind that understands the machine holistically—in empirical as well as theoretical terms—can diagnose problems that may exist in the computer or in the relationship between the computer and the machine.

These points were made a few months earlier as I watched Willie tune a car in which a customer had installed new ignition parts only to find that the car ran worse afterward.

Willie first checks for mistakes in the installation of the new parts. Finding none, he starts the engine and removes each spark plug wire from the distributor, noting the color and intensity of the spark that leaps between the wire and its orifice. It is a standard method.

Willie next checks the fuel distribution system. The wires to the fuel injectors on each cylinder are removed one at a time, and the engine balks in precisely the same fashion in each case, suggesting that the fuel is being properly fed to the engine. Since each subsystem is working correctly, the problem has to be in the relationship between them.

Willie puts his hand on an adjustment for the computer input, up by the firewall of the car. With his other hand he adjusts the air intake to the whole system. He loosens the distributor and moves it in relation to the adjustments to the two other inputs, but it does not produce the expected effect on either. Willie's mood brightens almost imperceptibly. He seems to be on to something.

*With a small **L**-shaped screwdriver he removes a second set of points that lie out of sight on the lower side of the distributor casing. He finds a clean paper towel, and we walk to the front of the shop to work in the soft, diffused light coming through the translucent plastic door panels. Carefully he cleans the connections in the points. When a small speck is left on the clean paper he looks up, pleased. He reinstalls the injector points, and now the adjustments make immediate and dramatic differences. The three elements are adjusted in relation to each other, one set of adjustments influencing all the rest, until he is satisfied. Now the engine idles quietly and evenly and surges when the accelerator is advanced.*

Later we talk about the repair. Willie begins: "On an electronic system—you've got an air intake you can adjust just like a diesel has. You've got to make sure your sensors are working. That's all you can repair on some of them, because your systems are sealed. Remember when you were having trouble with your truck in the fall—with the electronic ignition? We couldn't go into that box to see what was wrong with it—it was sealed. Now if they made those so you could get into them, they wouldn't make money on selling them, because you could get into them and repair them."

"Would you say the knowledge of that mechanic who works with the computer is as good as the knowledge of the mechanic who fixed this stuff without a diagnostic machine? Does the computer make your kind of mechanic obsolete?"

"No," Willie answers, "there's still a place for a good mechanic. But most of them have machines where they more or less just plug a car into it now. Most of your cars come through now with the lights right in the dash to tell you when something goes wrong."

"Does that make the kind of mechanic you are obsolete?"

"No, not really." Then Willie seems to contradict himself: "You've got a unit you hook onto the car, plus you've got a computer readout on the car itself. You could take a book and go right through it. It's all laid out in the book, your

88 Diagnosing an engine knock.

directions on how to go, what to check, and everything. Same as the Saab has on the computer box—you check it step by step. Troubleshooting with the computer."

"But before you had the computer you had to rely on your . . . intuition, your sight, your sound . . ."

". . . your *sense*. The computer's taking over the sense the mechanic used to have."

"That's what I meant by becoming obsolete," I say. "Does the new mechanic not have to have that sense any more?"

"If he wants to be a mechanic he's got to take a little schooling on it—be a little educated on how to use the computers. But he's got to be a little mechanically inclined to do it right. If you're not mechanically inclined you can't put the computer knowledge to use.

"They say you've got to have a computer to check whether a car's in tune or not, but that doesn't always work. Look at Ray Dean there—the trouble he's had with his new Chevy. It's taken him nine months to find out one little problem that was in his carburetor. I told him that to start with. 'It's under warranty—they've got to take care of it,' he says. He kept running right back to Chevrolet there in Canton. The computer light in his car kept coming on, but they couldn't find the problem."

"How did you know what it was?"

"The sound of the engine. The way it was running. I could have fixed it in five minutes.

"It reminds me of the car I tuned last month when you were in the garage. The points for the fuel injection—they had oil film—that's all that was wrong with them. Now that oil film on the injector points, the computer won't pick that up. I've got the analyzer here that's supposed to pick all that up, but it doesn't. You've got to listen to a number of things at one time, and it takes a period of time to pick that up. You don't learn it overnight. Like when I was learning aviation mechanics. The guy who taught says, 'Some of you boys will go out of here mechanics, and some of you will go out of here as parts exchangers— you'll never be a mechanic.' It's a type of knowledge that you can pick up and store in your mind. Quite a difference in the two. And we've got more parts exchangers around here than we've got mechanics."

SUMMARY

The kinesthetic sense infuses all of the work. Married to the knowledge of materials, it produces a working knowledge that stands in stark contrast to the work-

89 Setting ignition tolerances.

ing knowledge produced by formal education. The kinesthetic quality of Willie's working method shows how his shop is premodern, a multidimensional dialectic of the theoretical and the empirical. Willie's training has been informal and years-long, and it has trained the hand and the eye as well as the mind. The result is more than the sum of its parts. It seems mysterious to those who do not have it. Working without such knowledge, a mechanic fights materials rather than communicating—reading their messages. The kinesthetic knowledge may be the hardest to attain because it is not easily reduced to the written word and cannot be gained through intellectual means. Gaining the kinesthetic sense, however, reduces the gap between the subject—the worker—and the object—the work. Pirsig goes so far as to say that "the absence of subject-object duality . . . is so well understood as folklore, common sense, the everyday understanding of the shop" (1974, 296).

Work and Time

Country music blares from the radio of the eighteen-wheeler parked on the road by Willie's shop. The owner is an unknown heavyset man who is waiting for a welding job on the rear frame of his truck. One of Willie's regular customers, a fifty-five-year-old woman who looks twenty years younger and drives a rare new Saab, waits for an oil change. Her first words, "Have you got that filter, Willie?" bring the answer, "I don't know—I haven't looked." She looks peeved; she's made an appointment, and she feels she deserves Willie's time. Willie winks at me as he pulls the oil filter off the shelf in the back room. I've come to repair the tiller and centerboard of a sailboat I've been working on for two summers. Dick Green works alone on a garden tractor parked in the bed of his pickup.

I work alone, with short moments of help when I get stuck. Willie leaves with someone to bring a small bulldozer to the shop. The woman with the new Saab is getting frustrated, and the man waiting for the welding says, "That Willie don't care at all for time." I say that I think Willie has something figured out. Five, ten, fifteen people a day wait for Willie, but he's never hurried. He never scrambles around. The important things get done. The woman says, "Yeah, maybe that's why I take seven pills a day for high blood pressure. But Willie's had my daughter's '68 Saab out here for a year waiting for an engine job," she says, changing her mind. "I know, I know, and I agree," I say; "but I guess she's getting around somehow?" "Her father bought her a Volkswagen in the meantime, and unfortunately I told Willie." "I think Willie knows when something is important," I say. "He's helped me when I've needed it, when I've really needed it. And more than once." Her mood changes. "And for me too," she says. "Once at 9:30 on a Saturday night he drove all the way to Potsdam to get me going . . . but I still wish my daughter was driving a Saab instead of a Volkswagen."

Willie returns; he moves the woman's Saab into position and quickly changes the oil. In the meantime he aligns the hood so it shuts properly and adjusts the fuel injection to smooth out the slow-speed idle. The woman brags about changing her oil every two thousand miles and expresses her appreciation for the small details of Willie's attention. The trucker becomes part of every conversation by talking about how much various parts of his truck cost. When the woman talks about oil, he says, "My oil changes cost 175 bucks. Filter alone costs 150." "See," Willie says to the woman, "you're getting a deal."

They settle for less than ten dollars, and she leaves. "Quite a looker," the trucker says to me. "Yeah," I answer, "and she's nearly sixty." He can't quite believe it. "She's got a kid thirty years old," I say. He doesn't answer but remains perched on the tire of a small bulldozer Willie has begun to disassemble. By now the trucker has accepted the pace of the day and is waiting his turn.

I get Willie to organize the spraying operation for my centerboard before he settles into the welding job on the eighteen-wheeler. He sprays one side of the centerboard, then prepares the welding job on the trucker's rig. When the centerboard is dry, instead of bothering Willie I turn it around to spray the other side. I put the paint on too heavily, and a sagged line forms across the middle of the centerboard. Willie is watching from behind the truck, twenty feet away. "If you like those lace curtains, why did you sand the others off?" he asks. "I know, I fucked it up," I answer. "To each their own profession," he says, getting in the final word. The work begins on the trucker's rig, until Willie pauses to deal with yet another man who has arrived looking for parts to fix the differential in his logging rig. As I prepare to leave, the trucker's radio is still playing away, a Merle Haggard song about America. On that Saturday everyone's work will get finished.

Time is a constant feature of modern work.[14] Willie's sense of time is different from the sense of time that pervades most tasks, and understanding this difference tells a lot about his work.

Repair work, in the "rationalized" repair shop, is similar to the work of production. In fully rationalized mass production, the mind and the hand have been separated. The worker uses only his or her hands; the intelligence of the work has been extracted from the productive process and given over to other strata in the division of labor—the human engineers who design the work processes and the managers who control them. With the separation of the work into mental and menial components, separation or *duality* also exists between the worker and the object of the work. This is a familiar image that does not need further development here. [15] Certainly the repairman uses more intelligence than does the assembly person, because he or she must interpret directions and transform them into reasonably skilled handwork. With time studies of repair, however (carried out by management in large shops or corporations to rationalize costs), and the resulting standardization of repair work, repair has come to fundamentally resemble mass production assembly work. The repairman in a rationally organized shop follows directions that were written when the repair was rationally defined rather than actions of his or her own design. The directions that guide the repair rest on the assumption that repair, like assembly, can be characterized as motions that have a "typical" duration.

An organization can compute labor costs of repair the same way it computes the labor costs of production. In the experience of work, activity is no longer the mediation between an individual and the object of attention; rather activity is taken out of the free-flowing context and passed through a grid of time determination. This separation of time from the flow of activity changes the experience of work. The repairman comes to work "by the clock" because he is accountable to the clock as it is embodied in managerial superiors.

Furthermore, the objectification of time in repair has brought repair under the control of management. The productivity of workers can then be assessed in terms of quantity (how much is done in relation to expected shop time) instead of the quality of the individual problem solving in each job. Ironically, as repair becomes more "parts changing" and less problem solving, there is less "quality" in the work, both with which to prove oneself and through which one can be evaluated. The work of repair becomes one-dimensional rather than many-dimensional.

These changes make it possible to organize repair on an ever-increasing scale. Owner-operated garages or shops are replaced by large service centers that are often branches of corporations as large as Sears or Chevrolet.

The imposition of modern time management on repair has also made the relationship between the customer and the repairman less of a face-to-face interaction based on common understanding and trust (the kind of relationship one traditionally had with one's medical doctor, for example), and more of a contractual agreement between individual and corporation. In the traditional relationship, reputation figured highly. The repairman was called on to prove the worth of his services and the justness of his price—*his* determination of the appropriate time of a particular job—each time a job was finished.

Trust between the customer and the repairman (or perhaps better, ongoing negotiation, since the customer may take the work to a different shop next time around) that the repairman will fix only what is broken (and all that is broken) and charge reasonably for his time is replaced by a relatively anonymous contract between an individual and a representative of one of the shops that all charge roughly the same price for what comes to be seen as the same job. The customer does not discuss the repair with the individual who performs it because there really is not much to discuss. The contract is set by the corporation—the cost of the repair has been determined by studies of typical repairs in the past, and the rate of the shop time is not negotiable. The customer gives up face-to-face negotiation for the expectation that the work bought will be *standard*—that is, precisely the repair the shop manual indicates as taking a predetermined length of time. Because many repairs are done while an automobile is still under warranty (another way time imposes itself on the nature of work), the costs of the repair become part of the general costs of large automotive corporations. Cars are, in fact, often traded in (and so recycled to a lower social class) when their warranties expire. The standardized repairs, then, are more characteristically done for those who buy new cars.

These are some of the ways time has become part of modern repair. The way time is experienced by Willie, who performs tasks for sale—and his customers—who buy Willie's time in often uncharacteristic ways—is interesting partly because it differs from what has become, for most, the typical experience of time in buying services.

Willie determines the durational aspect[16] of his time life. This means that he maintains control over his time, letting activities determine informal schedules rather than allowing schedules to dictate his activities. One of the keys to understanding Willie's work is see how it is free from time as we usually define it. Time does not impose itself, forcing the work along at an "unnatural" pace. The pace is set by the natural power and rhythm of the body (which varies) and the particular quality of "attention" a job requires. That this makes Willie's work distinctive is made clear by Zerubavel: "The drift of civilization is an increasing detachment from organic and functional periodicity, which is dictated by nature, and its replacement by 'mechanical periodicity', which is dictated by the schedule, the calendar, and the clock."[17]

Time is thought of in terms of the activity of work rather than as a constraining context into which work must be placed. In this way time is embedded in activity; the specific nature of the job determines the duration of the work. This has two sides in a situation where one's time is for sale.

First, people generally expect services to be bought in fairly explicit terms. This is due in part to the drift away from "trust," or ongoing negotiation between repairman and customer in a face-to-face situation, to a more purely contractual arrangement through which services are bought and sold. If you buy Willie's time, however, you must trust that he will assign a "fair" dollar value to what you have bought. You may have actually purchased more time, and I suppose it is possible that you may have purchased less time. The important issue is that Willie determines the value of the time sold.

People generally like to know when their jobs are going to be finished. This is especially true, of course, if they are building their own schedules around the use of a machine that is being repaired, but beyond that it is simply a function of the degree to which we make each other accountable for time and schedules. Because Willie's time sense differs so radically from what has become the accepted time-as-money consciousness, many people take their work elsewhere rather than adapt. And because time in the shop is mandated by the work and the jobs are often more complex than parts changing, work often takes longer than Willie or customers expect. Willie is often "behind"; customers nearly always want their work done sooner than they get it. But Willie does not adjust his experience of time to the close accounting of a time-for-sale shop. And though there is an hourly rate posted on the wall (as required by the state), he figures the cost of his work based on many variables, of which the actual time spent working is but one.

The quality of work that attracts people to Willie's shop derives in part from the fact that it is not influenced by outside constraints such as time (and one senses in a related manner, money). Willie does not rush through one job to get to the next. He does not do extra work (adding shop time) to make more money. The embedding of time in the work means that attention is entirely focused on the work activity rather than on the time that work is taking. This leads to a much different quality of attention, and thus a different quality of work. Time and attention are linked; good work results.

All examples of Willie's work document, sometimes indirectly, these particular qualities of time in the shop. I will, however, illustrate these ideas in a single example that touches many of the themes introduced above.

Caliper

A week before Christmas, a loud screeching when I apply the brakes tells me the asbestos lining has worn off the brake pads and the metal underneath is scraping on the wheel disk. If the car is driven this way for long the disk will be gouged and ruined. I call Willie to ask if he has a set of pads: "Maybe not new ones," he answers, "but something to get you going!" Usually the brakes on one wheel of a pair wear out first; both sides of the front or back pair are replaced, and Willie saves the pads that are not completely worn out. I arrange to do the work the next morning, a day I am supposed to be preparing grant proposals for a deadline a day away, hassling at United Parcel Service along with everyone else who has yet to ship Christmas packages, and writing course outlines and ordering books for the coming semester. I sense time pushing hard in my life, but I reason that the job at Willie's shouldn't take more than an hour, and I should be able to do it alone.

I'm hoping to work inside the shop because the outside temperature hovers at three above zero, but all the berths are filled. Willie is on the last stages on a job that has taken six months, but he says it will be completed that morning, clearing a berth for me.

The job Willie finishes is a conversion from automatic to manual transmission in a ten-year-old Saab. The body and interior of the car are in remarkable condition. The automatic transmission, however, stopped working a month after the car's new owner began driving it. Willie was to install a used manual transmission he salvaged from a wreck. The replacement transmission had to be rebuilt, the engine compartment modified to accept the new transmission, linkage and pedals installed, and the ignition system modified. It was a job that was difficult in subtle ways, and for a number of reasons such as missing parts or more pressing problems in other jobs the project had been stalled again and again. At a party a month before I'd met the owner's wife, who had moved to the area from Southern California. She had expressed incomprehension, frustration, and anger over the stalled job. Everything she said was perfectly reasonable given people's typical expectations about buying services. I had no way to explain the situation to her; she was not interested in rural anthropology, only in getting the car fixed. Then either you put up with it or you don't, I said. No one else would do the job even if they were able, because it was so frustrating, and very few people would have the skill, let alone the willingness. The owner of the car, a man who had grown up in the North Country, focused on what Willie was doing rather than the pace of the job. When he stopped by the shop to check progress he was never impatient, never demanding. As Willie kept uncovering new problems, the owner told Willie to fix them all. So as the job went on and on it became a restoration rather than simple replacement. But it became a sore point even for Willie, and when he said one day, "He's been more patient than he should have had to be—more patient than I'd have been!" it was an admission I'd never heard before.

One day when I was at the shop the Saab's owner stopped by and mentioned that the engine ran roughly. Willie disassembled the engine and installed new rod bearings. During the job he fixed the timing-chain tightener, which had been improperly installed. The starter switch had been broken and replaced by a push-button starter, and the wiring had shorted out in two circuits. Willie fixed the wiring and installed a used ignition switch when the floor pan was removed to install the linkage for the shift lever. The day before I came to fix my brakes Willie had test-driven the car and discovered that the heater didn't work, so he salvaged a heater box from a wreck and installed it, a job that had taken most of the morning. Now everything was finished except the emergency brake, which had set up in the front wheels. The wheels would have to be disassembled to free them up.

Willie is working on a front wheel when I arrive to begin my brake job. He has discovered that the ball joints, part of the front suspension, are worn out. He doesn't have the new parts, but he tells me there is a wreck in a snowbank outside the shop that the parts can be salvaged from. I am drawn into the work to get to mine more quickly.

Willie shows me how to approach the two large nuts that hold the ball joints in place. The parts I seek, inside the front wheel wells of the wreck, look like rusted pieces of junk, and the nuts holding them in place are fused onto their bolts. How superior it would be, I think as I try without success to break the nuts loose, to walk into the parts department, take down two new pieces burnished smooth and silvery, threads clean, all internal parts guaranteed to work! I recall a conversation with myself at that moment—New parts don't exist in this shop; the old parts will probably work; and until I get the rusty nuts off this wreck, Brown's car won't get finished and mine will remain unfixed. The end I sought, new brakes for my car, would be accomplished only if quality attention could be focused on the means to that end—getting four rusty nuts off their bolts.

I rap the part sharply with a five-pound hammer, and the nuts begin to give. But the lock nuts come off slowly, with no lessening of pressure. I push with all my strength (working on my knees in the snow, bent over into the wheel well) for an eighth of a turn.

Halfway through the first of four nuts I return to the shop to warm my hands. Willie has been trying for half an hour to remove a bolt that holds the brake caliper onto Brown's wheel hub to expose the emergency brake underneath. He's applied heat, used penetrating oil, and given the bolt a few good raps, but it will not come loose. If he breaks the bolt the whole wheel will have to be taken apart and the broken stud burned out of the hole—a job that will take a couple of hours at least.

I return to my job and finish removing the ball joints, which are, as Willie had predicted, in good condition. But when I return to the shop with my work completed Willie holds up the piece of stud that, for all his careful work, he's broken off the caliper. The other part of the stud remains in the caliper and will have to be removed. His half-hour job is up to an hour, and it will be another two hours at least before it will be finished. Later we discuss the photographs I took of the afternoon's work.

90 Burning off the penetrating oil.

91 Drilling through the broken stud, being careful not to hit the threads.

Willie begins, "I was drilling out a bolt that broke off that holds a brake caliper. I usually drill the hole through, and then it's easier to heat and blow out without blowing the rest of the metal out—yup [Willie looks at other photos in series]—that's what I did.

"That was a transmission job for Don Brown—we put him another transmission in—we went from an automatic to a shift. We started making it roadworthy, and we found that the ball joints were worn out and the brakes had problems, too."

"You were fooling with that bolt for quite a bit of time while I was outside."

"Trying to get it out without breaking it—it didn't work."

Willie says, "You've got to get the broken piece out of the caliper assembly. You drill through it [91] so the heat will go all the way through the hole, so you can get your quick heat to where you don't blow [to apply intense heat from the cutting torch] the rest of the metal away that's not the bolt. The torch almost blows the bolt threads and everything right out of the material threads that are left there. This way you run a tap through—clean it out—it's all set. But it's tricky. You've got to concentrate or you lose it. If you blow the wrong spot you ruin the whole spindle and you have to put another one on."

92 Drilling out the broken stud in the brake caliper.

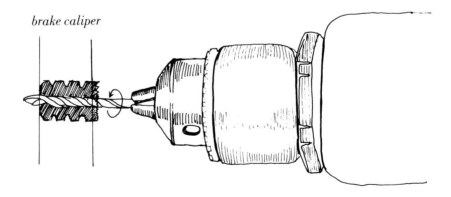

brake caliper

I ask if he could drill a hole, run a tap directly through, and be left with a threaded hole.

"Not as tight as that was, you couldn't. You had to blow it out. If you don't have a torch you drill it as close as you can and hope that the tap will clean 'em. It doesn't do as good a job, though, because you can mess up the threads that's already in it if you don't get it started in the right position. You don't have to blow the whole thing. I don't like to blow any more of it than I have to—you spoil the threads if you get too close—if you get it too hot. That's a small piece of metal, and it heats up fast. You have to take your time at it. The surrounding area heats up pretty fast too.

"I was working it with penetrating oil, but it wouldn't free it up. That's why you see such a flame on it [90]—the penetrating oil was burning off. I was cleaning it off so it didn't flare up and give me any trouble on seeing what I was doing. See, if you've got the oil on there and you hit it and try to heat it it'll give you a flame, and it's pretty hard to see through that flame. So you more or less just dry it off.

"You've got two settings on the torch, one for heating and one for blowing the metals. If your metals aren't hot enough they won't blow. When you're heating it up you can have the torch at an angle, but if you blew on an angle that is how the hole would be—you'd take part of the caliper with it."

"The angle of the torch didn't make sense to me when I was making that photograph [90]."

"See, oil got in behind the back plate, and on the front side of it, too. That's why you've got flame on both the front and back of the plate [90]. The sparks are different when I touch the oxygen onto it to blow it. But when I touched the oxygen to blow it you didn't have much of a chance to take a picture of it— that's quick. [Willie looks back through the photos.] No, by God, you did get it—you didn't get it all but you got most of it."

"You see here [93] I've dropped down to the lower side of the hole, cutting, and I'm working around on it. You can just see the very edge of the bolt there, where it's hot [top of circle where flames are coming out—a faint white crescent shape]. And you've got to hit that quick because if you don't the rest of the metal heats and comes with it. Then you've got to replace the whole thing."

93 Blowing through the broken stud.

"This is running the tap through the hole [94]," Willie says, "and photo 95 is the point of the whole job—the hole with the threads still in it—with the broken stud out."

I comment, "Those are the kinds of things that are easy to get stuck in. You give yourself a certain amount of time to do a job, and then you end up spending hours just trying to get started; just trying to get the first bolt out."

Willie answers, "Oh, you can break bolts and still know what you're doing. If you break it off you've got to get it out."

Later I asked Willie what he charged for everything he had done to Brown's car. When he told me the price, less than the cost of a new transmission, I mentioned that I thought it was pretty low, considering the hours all the small jobs had required. He said, "Oh, I couldn't charge for all I did—the car's not worth it!" In a general sense it was true; the market value of the car would be less than the cost of the hours spent and the parts Willie installed. One must ask, then, why Willie proceeded, apparently unconcerned about these issues, for the duration of the job. I think the answer lies in an attitude that sees the imperatives of the work ahead of the relation between time and money. Willie's work provides identity; it is the re-creation of self. He must, however, derive his material as well as his psychological sustenance from the work; money must be earned to keep his family together and the shop in operation. But the price is assigned, in jobs like this restoration from which a small chapter has been described, from a *general* rather than a specific sense of what the job is worth. In this case it does not add up to all the separate "times" of the work. It is also important to recall, in the bumper job on the Ford tractor, Willie's comment that rebuilding the original grille would "take more time than it's worth." Clearly there is a time/money consciousness, but it is not the kind of accounting that characterizes typical production or modern repair work.

The quality of time I observe in the work is integral to the quality of attention Willie gives to extracting a broken bolt. To many the broken bolt would be only a source of frustration, another detour to an end typically seen as the money one receives for the completed repair. To Willie the broken caliper bolt is simply one more unit of time, one more *means* on which attention is focused, leading to the completed job. The customer was probably not even told of this episode in the long process.

I think that the pressure of schedules in my own life, which sometimes leads to anxiety and to low-quality work and low-quality experience, made the day at Willie's particularly telling. Once I could realize that the work mandated the day's time rather than vice versa, the work could be seen in terms of its particular

94 Running the tap through the blown hole to clean out the threads.

95 The brake caliper with the broken stud removed.

challenges and rewards. In this way Willie's shop is an escape from modernity, an escape from the externally imposed schedules that impinge on even the briefest moments of experience. Willie's apparent peace of mind derives from his owner-ship of his time, the concentration of means, rather than ends, in the activity of life.[18] Pirsig suggests that in the shop where this type of work is typical, there is a fusion of what he calls "romantic" and "classical" quality:

"You can actually *see* this fusion in skilled mechanics and machinists of a certain sort, and you can see it in the work they do. To say they are not artists is to misunderstand the nature of art. They have patience, care and attentiveness to what they're doing, but more than this—there's a kind of inner peace of mind that isn't contrived but results from a kind of harmony with the work in which there's no leader and no follower. The materials and the craftsman's thought change together in a progression of smooth, even changes until his mind is at rest at the exact instant the material is right." (1974, 296)

Time is in work; duality disappears.

Summary

I arrived to find Willie alone in the shop, reassembling the front axle of an eighty-five-horse-power International tractor. It is a job I would have expected to see in a garage for heavy equipment, with hydraulic lifts and plenty of help. The seat of the tractor was above eye level; the rear wheels were the height of a grown man. By Willie's estimate the axle and the front wheels, which he had removed and fixed, weighed well over five hundred pounds.

Two small jacks supported the four-ton tractor's front end. The jacks by them-selves did not extend far enough to raise the tractor body to the proper height to meet the wheels—one jack sat on an elm log and the other on a precarious-looking pile of pine two-by-fours. If the tractor rolled back or ahead just a little it would tip off the jacks and crash to the concrete floor. One of the jacks was leaning slightly, and the tractor was creaking backward. We quickly put other jacks behind each of the back wheels, propped into the heavy thread at a forty-five-degree angle, to act as wheel blocks. We pumped those jacks just the slightest bit to roll the wheels ahead and bring the front jacks perpendicular to the floor again.

The owners of the tractor had twisted and broken the front axle housing, a five-foot tube six inches in diameter, by driving into a frozen manure pile. Willie had straightened the tube, welded it back together, and welded a "Band-Aid" of metal on top of the welded crack. The welding was relatively straightforward; the difficult part of the job was straightening the tube. Willie welded on more metal because the axle was not, in his view, made of heavy enough material.

Willie had reattached the wheels to the rebuilt axle before I arrived. To finish the job we had only to position the front wheel assembly and bolt it into place. Each three-foot-high wheel weighed about two hundred pounds, since they were filled with liquid to weight down the front of the tractor. The front wheels, mounted on the axle, were free to flop sideways. Unlike automobile wheels, they were connected to the axle with a universal joint that permitted them to tip and bend as the tractor was driven over steep hills and gulleys. It made the wheel assembly almost impossible to move, because the wheels had to be kept from falling sideways as they were rolled ahead.

We balanced the wheel assembly and inched it back, over to the side, and up to the correct height. Willie nudged, pried with long steel pipes, jacked and lowered, and slowly positioned the assembly while I balanced and steadied the wheels and axle. A single pin attached the assembly to the tractor. As we moved the assembly into place it had to be kept from falling sideways and knocking the tractor off the jacks. When we finally had the pieces in line the pin slipped in, and our hour-long concentration broke into minor euphoria. It seemed that we had been pushed to our limits, but then I realized that if I had not happened by Willie would have done the job by himself.

The job that had brought the tractor to the shop was finished, but Willie did not stop working. One front tire was bald because the alignment mechanism had never been adjusted. The inward-directed wheel also made the tractor difficult to steer. The alignment is set by extending or shortening a bar that connects the wheels and keeps them parallel. The bar is extended or shortened with an adjustable sleeve. A bolt passes through the sleeve and through a groove in the bar to keep the two pieces from slipping. The trouble with the tractor was that the grooves on the bar were in the wrong place. If you put the bolt through the closest groove the wheels would toe in; but using the next groove, they would toe out. Willie took the assembly apart (loosening the rusted bolts first with his torch, then with 808, and finally breaking them loose with a three-foot ratchet) and cut a groove in the right place with his air grinder. When he reassembled the mechanism the wheels were in line for the first time in the tractor's existence. He started the tractor up and drove it ahead twenty feet and then back, maybe three times, and with his hands off the steering wheel the newly aligned wheels kept the tractor moving in a straight line. He certainly wouldn't make money for fixing the steering. He probably wouldn't even mention it, since these customers were the type to complain about work they hadn't asked for. The whole incident wasn't a huge thing, yet it represented a typical attitude in the shop toward the work. Repair becomes restoration. The satisfaction Willie gained from making the tractor right was his payment.

Willie's method can be summed up as an inductive approach fueled by attention, patience, and creativity. I've talked about the role of the setting; the idea that a certain kind of environment requires its own form of survival, which for some becomes a working method. I've shown how Willie's attitude and method are similar to those of people who made and repaired things centuries ago. I've suggested that Willie's working knowledge is due in part to the way he learned—informally, from his own kin, throughout the years of his maturation. The working knowledge depends on a deep and thorough knowledge of materials. The working method depends on a certain attitude toward time stated most modestly as patience, most dramatically as a kind of contemplative attitude that sees all steps to an end as equal. The working method is a combination of small steps of hypothesis forming and testing through which many inductive strings lead to deductive generalities that launch more inductive experiments. It depends on a kind of kinesthetic knowledge that is difficult to describe, close as it is to the actual flow of experience. In these ways I've "disassembled" Willie's method, but I feel I've also dismembered it. While I am satisfied that each of these ideas describes part of Willie's working knowledge, the parts do not seem to equal the whole. I am frustrated with the old problem of translating human experience into words. But I also have the feeling that I've left something out. While I might have described all the relevant elements, I have not described the glue that holds them together—the quality that is the most essential of all.

That essential element is, I believe, what Thorstein Veblen, in 1914, called the instinct of workmanship. Veblen believed this was fundamental to all human action. The instinct of workmanship fulfills a human tendency to "seek realization and expression in an unfolding activity"—an impulse to constructive action. I interpret Willie's work and its setting in the same way Veblen interpreted his own pioneer background. Veblen's father was a skilled craftsman, a farmer, and an intellectual, and his mother was an amateur doctor on the western frontier in the middle of the nineteenth century. His parents, able to manage their challenging material environment and still maintain a life of the mind, resembled the Icelandic farmer/poet/craftsman—the bricoleur, I am tempted to say—that Veblen implicitly celebrates in the introduction to his translation of *The Laxdaela Saga* (1925). Veblen's biting criticisms of industrial capitalism, of conspicuous consumption, of vacuous patriotism, of higher education transformed by business ethics, were all balanced with his fundamental view of humans as naturally purposive. He writes: "The instinct [to workmanship] may be in some sense . . .

concerned with the ways and means of life rather than with any one given ulterior end. It has essentially to do with proximate rather than ulterior ends. Yet workmanship is not the less an object of attention and sentiment in its own right. Efficient use of the means at hand and adequate management of the resources available for the purposes of life is itself an end of endeavour, and accomplishment of this kind a source of gratification" (in Lerner 1948, 318).

To suggest fundamental qualities of the human animal, as Veblen has done, is essentially an exercise in social philosophy. The tradition, however, has always been a part of social analysis. Veblen never lost his belief in the human-as-maker, though he saw the various forms of his ideal type alienated by the institutional forms these "instincts" realized. Willie has the instincts of workmanship, perhaps because he is isolated from the main institutional forms of modern social life. But whatever the reason the form persists, its roots are deep in the traditions of Western culture.

Part 2   CONTEXTS OF WORK

Work and the Environment

Willie's personal values and his role in the community come from his work. The contexts of work are in his mind and in his community. Although these dimensions are extremes of a continuum, in Willie's case they are intimately related. The individual and the community are consistent in tone and content.

Willie's personal values, broadly stated, concern the proper use of machines and material. Willie values material and machines in terms of their usefulness and their exchange value in a partly barter economy. The value of materials and objects has only a slight relation to their original market value.

Willie's values also guide his actions with others. In general he deals with people as he deals with machines. There are seldom flashy repairs; personal relationships are built with the same methodical pace and attention to detail that most of his mechanical work requires. Just as machines are maintained for a long time and often readapted over the course of their usefulness, so people stay in Willie's universe for a long time, though his relationships with them may change. The long process of interaction leads to reputation—the community's perception of a person's actions. But the process of reputation building is complex—first Willie's work creates self-definition; the sense of self then guides actions that are, over time, perceived, accepted, or rejected by others. Reputation is never totally achieved; rather, it is a process of ongoing actions and self-proclamations before the ever-watchful eye of others in one's community.

Reputation leads to social power. But it is a social power that is by no means objective or unquestioned. The community continually redefines the social power around the rise and fall of reputations, such as that emerging from all the deals that move through Willie's shop. Because Willie's business world is a mixture of formal contracts and implicit understandings, many of the deals are fraught with conflict, and many are never resolved. Willie's frequent storytelling presents his side of these conflicts. Because he is known for good work and honest dealing, his accounts usually stick. And because Willie's work is invariably needed, even by those who sometimes take advantage when they have the chance, he gains a kind of moral power to define what kinds of actions are proper in the community.

I have suggested that Willie's values arise from his work. This is not a startling insight. In fact, nearly all anthropologists who watch and listen to people and then learn about what they believe make the connection between ideas and material circumstances. Bensman and Lilienfeld suggest we look specifically at occupations as a source of personal beliefs: "It is our contention that major 'habits of mind,' approaches to the world, or in phenomenological terms, attitudes towards everyday life, and specialized attitudes, are extensions of habits of thought that emerge and are developed in the practice of an occupation, profession, or craft. We emphasize craft since we focus upon the methods of work, techniques, methodologies, and the social arrangements which emerge in the practice of a profession as being decisive in the formation of world views" (1973, 1). Bensman and Lilienfeld's contribution is particularly useful because while they see the world of work as the source of knowledge—ideas, attitudes, "habits of mind"—they expand upon the idea that social class, defined as one's relationship to the means of production, is the determining category from which we may understand specific ideas and values.[1] They suggest that only in a general way does social class determine social ideas, and that one must look specifically at occupations and, within occupations, at specific techniques and methods to see the relationship between ideas and their settings.

Bennett Berger has developed the "microsociology of knowledge" in his study of how ideas such as specific norms relate to their settings—families, friendship networks, or work groups—in his research on the "ideological work" of rural communards.[2] He stresses the dialectical relationship between ideas and their changing material contexts as he shows how a group of rural hippies evolved new definitions of their love lives, their child-rearing practices, and their overall view of living on the land as the conditions of their lives changed. Berger's microsociology of knowledge, given the detail with which it presents both the "moral ideologies" and the circumstances related to the group's existence, is good instruction for studying Willie's work and values. Berger does not minimize the complexity, the tensions, or the contradictions in the relation of ideas to circumstances. Ideas are to be understood in terms of their material contexts, but the relationship is complex, subject to change, and even under the best of conditions, only partly knowable.

Willie's ability to see value in things other people overlook is the basis for much of his work. The restoration of the Ford tractor described earlier illustrates this well. The general tendency to see value in the usefulness of material, however, goes beyond the examples described in the first section of the book.

For Willie "junk" cars are a storehouse of parts. It is not only the major components, such as engines and transmissions, that are valuable when a car is junked. The small parts, even brackets or fasteners, also have value far beyond their simple monetary worth. This is especially true for a mechanic like Willie who works almost exclusively on a single make of car. Twenty or thirty miscellaneous junked cars sitting outside a general mechanic's shop would be hard to use efficiently. Twenty to thirty old Saabs, however, constitute a cache of parts for a rather esoteric automobile. Saab parts are hard to find and expensive. Because the cars Willie fixes are often seven to fifteen years old, the parts needed may be

96 Willie's Saab heaven.

obsolete or unavailable—even just a bolt with a specific length and thread. But the part is "cataloged" on a car sitting outside, ready to be used. People who own old Saabs know that used parts are available at Willie's and that they will be relatively cheap. In this way Willie's business depends on having such parts on hand.

The value of the junked cars is limited, however. There comes a time when nearly everything of use has been stripped from a car. As we studied a photograph of the shop yard Willie remarked:

"Gilmore was supposed to come over and haul a lot of that stuff away—there's a lot of junk in there that's unnecessary. In the shop and out of the shop. That stuff out alongside of the driveway has got to be cleaned up, taken away. They get some money out of it by the weight at a junkyard. And some of it—they sort it and get a better price out of it. They'll sort through aluminum and cast [iron]—all your electric motors have got copper in them—they strip that out—better price out of it. There's money in the junk business—if a guy does it right and knows what he's doing. I've even got motor blocks laying inside there— V-4 motor blocks. It's no good! They blew a rod or something and broke the block—there's no sense in keeping that stuff. Crankshaft may be good; three pistons—but it's all been cleaned out. Block's just laying there. It's got to go."

To an outsider a shop like Willie's seems to be filled with junk. Junk, however, is material without value. When you understand how the shop operates, you see how use or exchange value comes out of the most unlikely objects. Willie salvages the value from all the material that comes through the shop; what is left over is junk, by his definition.

The brief passage and photo sequence that follow document one of scores of repairs I've observed in which Willie uses a part from a wreck outside the shop. In this repair Willie rebuilt the internal linkages in a windshield wiper mechanism with a number of parts he made himself. The wiper post, which extends through the body of the car, is threaded and held tight to the body with a large flat nut. Willie had installed the new linkages, but the nut that held the post was rusted into place. Unless the nut was replaced the wipers would again work their way out of alignment, and the linkages would eventually break. Willie cut the old nut off and retrieved one from a wreck outside the shop to finish the job.

"We were fixing an old repair that hadn't been done right. The housing for the wiper cable came loose. In fact, the little nuts came off on the inside—it's a two-piece housing. We had to fasten the cable back into the motor. But we

97 Cutting off a rusted nut
that holds the windshield
wiper post.

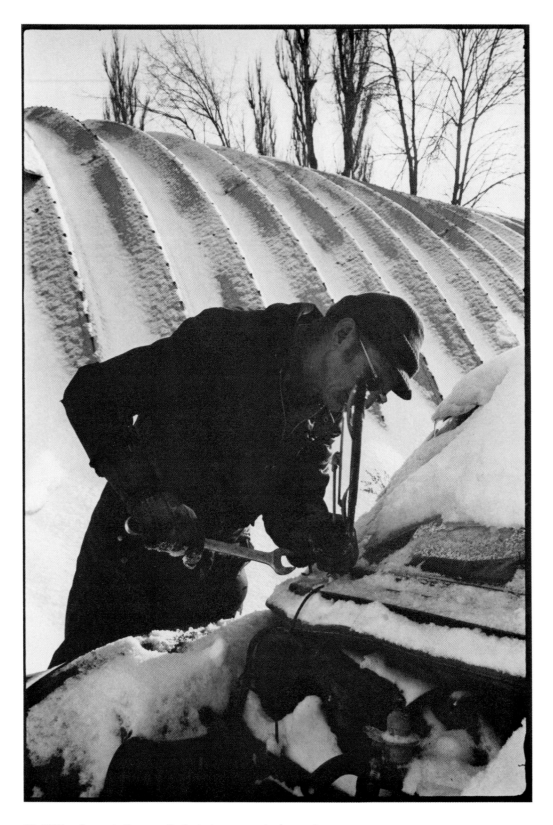

98 Willie takes a similar nut off a junked car to use in the repair.

couldn't tighten up the nut that held the post to the car. We had to cut that nut off, and I didn't have a spare. These kinds of jobs depend on going out and taking off a part when I need one. My spare parts are on all those car bodies. When you've got the cars sitting there you can go and get a small part, a bracket, or even a particular screw. If you tore them down and cataloged them I'd have to have a building bigger than my shop to put them in."

Pirating from the junkers that surround the shop salvages parts and material that would otherwise be wasted, saves money, and makes repair work more efficient. Willie maintains a mental catalog of parts available in the numerous cars around the shop, and he is generous in offering them at a low price, or no price at all, to customers who are working on their own projects. Finally, he often trades labor for junked cars to replenish his store of these parts. In total, the process is a recycling that extracts fuller use from a wide range of material.

The used parts and materials that surround the shop are useful beyond the repair of old Saabs. Willie used pieces he picked up around the shop, for example, to fix the Ford tractor I described earlier. The following discussion shows another example of how Willie sees the potential in these items. An important theme is how this material comes into the shop (and often leaves in new forms) through barter and other forms of exchange.

WILLIE: "This [99] is a Ford truck cab. It's laying in the driveway. This [lower right-hand corner] is a blade for the Jeep. Hot-water tank behind the blade. I'll take it apart and use the can out of it for tiling, or whatever a guy wants. A lot of farmers come in and get them split in half for hog troughs or for watering cows out in the field."

DOUG: "Where did that Ford cab come from?"

WILLIE: "A guy brought a truck in and wanted it cut down into a trailer. I made the trailer—that's the trailer I was using in the woods. Someday he'll come and pick it up. I cut the cab off, narrowed the frame up, and put a hitch on it. Then he gave me the front part of it for the work I did on the trailer. I'm going to make another trailer out of it. From the frame where it was cut off to make his trailer you've got your whole front end that carried the motor. You can make a trailer out of that too. Put a draw hitch on it—see, this is off the frame already. The other part sits up there in the parking lot."

DOUG: "It looks like he was getting a better deal than you were."

WILLIE: "Not really. He's one of these fellas—he does a lot for me. If I need something done and he knows I want it done and I'm not in too good a shape to do it—*he* does it. He wouldn't let me go onto my roof to put the shingles on—he did it. So it's one of these deals—well, I've known him, oh, thirty years, and his wife—I've known her ever since she was knee-high. You work with your friends and your neighbors and you work out a lot better. And I haven't got that much time tied up in it. They took the cab and cut it all loose. I told them how to do it, but they did all the cutting. I just helped them tip it off.

"I used it to haul all my stones—twenty-two tons on both banks—to the bridge. You helped on that. We nearly busted the bottom out of it. I hooked the little garden tractor on it and brought a load of wood up the other day. I got up along the house, and it didn't want to come up. Made three tries at it, on the ice. I said, 'Julie, sit on the drawbar.' She says, 'I'm not heavy enough for that.' I says [kind voice], 'Just sit on the drawbar. . . .' she crawled up on the drawbar and we tried it again. Walked right up—never spun a wheel."

Using one's land to store junked cars can be a touchy issue. At one level it is a confrontation between aesthetic and pragmatic values. In most areas of the country land must be zoned for it, and such lots must be hidden behind high fences. Willie's part of the North Country is only now undergoing land zoning. The issue pits the new residents, who often work in the towns and live in the country to experience the beauty of rural life, against those who live and work close to the land and use it in ways that are sometimes not very pretty. Not surprisingly, many people who have lived in the area all their lives view how they use their land as

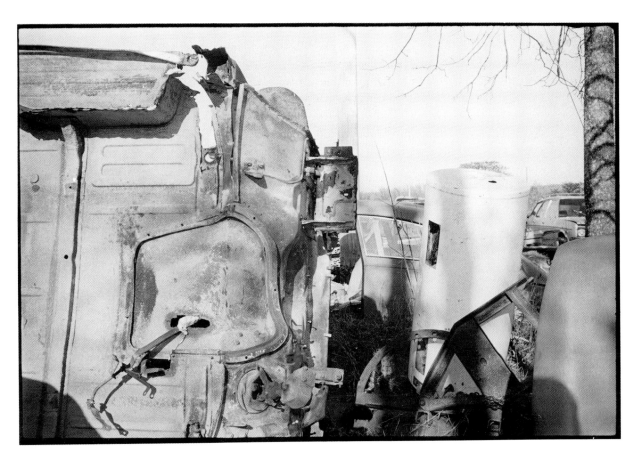

99 Ford truck cab near
Willie's shop.

their own business. Ironically enough, Willie is a strong advocate of zoning. It is not clear whether his way of life will have to change when the zoning system passes, since exceptions are made for those who have businesses in operation before zoning laws take effect, but his attitude implies an overall acceptance of a community-based law defining both the aesthetic and the pragmatic use of land.

WILLIE: "If the zoning goes through and a new shop gets set up they've got to live by the code. Your parking spaces have got to go according to the square footage of your building. And you're allowed two cars outside; only one can be there a year. You can't have any other cars around for parts or anything unless they're concealed. A guy could put up a building, similar to what I've got for a shop. Take the cars in there and conceal them. Now if I was out on Highway 345, which is a number 1 highway, those cars I have out there would have to have a fence around them. A board fence, or something to obstruct the view of them. But back on this road I don't have to. The same with the ones I've got down by the garden.

[Later in our conversation]: "You can be strict on the zoning and you can be too strict. Around here they're not strict enough. And about fifty years from now, if they don't get zoning in it ain't going to be worth living here. But it is starting to build back, compared to the way it used to be. A lot of the old buildings and things—they're getting rid of them—tearing them down. A few of the old barns are around yet, a few houses. Most of the sore-eyes are gone now. But they've taken out a few of the landmarks, which I'd like to see have stayed. This halfway schoolhouse, at the end of the road here. I tried and tried to get that, to fix it back original but still make living quarters in it. That would have been nice. Kept the name 'Halfway Schoolhouse' up on it. . . . They quit holding classes in it about thirty, thirty-five years ago. They sold that out—the guy who lived where Carl Froats lives now kept all the school records. According to Carl there's some of the old records in there yet. And right over here in Chamberlin Corners—that was a schoolhouse on the corner. The little one, across from the bridge. I tried to buy that one at one time.

[Still later]: "That's like down Highway 81, down almost into—I forget if it's Scranton or Wilkes Barre—you can travel for five, six mile. And one hillside, across from that, when you're traveling—it's all cars. All *old* cars. Just as far as you can see as you drive along. It's right on the whole mountainside. It's covered with cars. You've never seen that?"

DOUG: "I don't remember that, though I've driven on that road."

WILLIE: "There's millions of dollars worth of parts in there in antique cars. That place has been there for years. His grandfather had it before him. It's not concealed because it's far enough from the highway so they can't make him conceal it. And actually it's not a sore-eye. To look at it. Anyone that knows anything about automotive. You look at it and say 'Oh boy, what a sight.' It's *beautiful*. You've got all these different colored car bodies setting over there, dotting that mountainside. And it really is nice."

ECOLOGICAL VALUES

Willie's orientation toward seeing value in material gives his shop operation an ecological bent. His contribution as a fixer makes machines last far longer than they do in most settings. After they are worn out in their original form they are often transformed for new uses. This use of parts from junked machines saves money and the resources needed to manufacture new parts while at the same time preserving a form of fixing that is more challenging than "parts changing."

Often Willie takes a car in trade that is mechanically sound but, like many that are ten to fifteen years old, has a number of nicks and small dents in the body and tears in the upholstery. These cars are restored to their original function, if not their original patina. Willie sprays undercoating—a rubberized material that leaves a gently bumpy surface—on all the areas where he has repaired rusted metal or where the paint has worn or chipped off. He may, for example, spray undercoating all the way to the beltline of the car. After this has dried for a few days he sprays colored enamel over the entire car. The surface with the undercoating looks odd because we expect cars to be shiny and smooth rather than evenly dimpled. But the undercoated surfaces are tougher than an enameled surface alone. If a seat is broken or badly worn he will take one from a junked Saab, though it will probably be a different color. Willie ends up with a mechanically sound automobile with a few visual peculiarities—one that will provide good transportation for a small amount of money. This is quite different from recreating the original appearance of a "classic" car. Classic restorations require a different type of compulsiveness and a great deal of money, and they produce machines that will be used delicately. Willie's restorations begin at the mechanical level and move to the exterior. There are no hidden surprises.

Willie is alert to the machines he uses and the environment they service. This might include something as simple as the proper use of a chain saw on a cold day, which I learned after I ruined a chain by not letting the lubricating oil warm up enough before I began cutting. I later noticed that after Willie started his saw he pointed it downward. Only when oil began to spurt from the end of the blade, making a small black track in the snow, did he begin cutting. He explained that when the temperature is below zero the engine must run long enough to heat the blade oil, which is in a separate reservoir. It is a very simple idea, but it signals an understanding of how the machine responds to the environment and how its use must be modified when conditions change.

This type of understanding extends to virtually all machines. It was made clear in our discussion of a bulldozer I had photographed outside the shop:

"The guy didn't understand when it was supposed to be greased and when it wasn't, so he wore it right out. He greased it by the book instead of *when* it needed to be greased. Plus—he didn't know that when the tracks are froze you don't run 'em. If the rollers get froze—underneath—you'll run flat spots on the rollers that run the tracks.

"When you use it in the late fall or the winter, you've got to always make sure the rollers are free. You never park it with mud on it. If necessary you put it in a high gear and run it over pretty rough ground to shake the stuff off it. Run it on frozen ground, and it'll shake all the mud and everything off—if it isn't frozen on from the last time you ran it. What happened to that dozer was that the rollers had frozen fast and they didn't free up until they had heated it up running it. But it didn't have any lubrication all that time, and it ruined them."

Willie's ecological orientation is also reflected in his view of agricultural mechanization.[3] He is not a "back to the lander" who criticizes machine-driven agriculture because it uses large quantities of fossil fuels, pesticides, herbicides, and inorganic fertilizers. Willie's ideas about agriculture come from his work repairing farm machinery. It is not agricultural mechanization in itself that is at the core of the problem. Rather, Willie sees that smaller and less powerful machines have less impact on the land. Furthermore, with smaller machinery, the farmer is more likely to be attuned to what the machine is doing both to the land and, as it wears, to itself.

This idea is illustrated in the different approaches farmers use to keep their tractors from getting stuck while harvesting crops during the short, wet fall. Although Willie is not a farmer, he generally works in the woods in the fall, and he faces the same problems farmers do in keeping his machines from being mired. He replaced the standard four-inch wheels on the front of his Ford tractor with seven-inch-wide ovals. On the back he replaced the nine-inch tires with twelve-inch smooth ones. When the mud or snow requires it, Willie puts chains on the back tires. These changes, Willie says, are for flotation—to stay on top of the mud.

In general, farmers take the opposite strategy. Willie comments:

"The fluid in the tires is to give them more weight. More traction. But when you're in the mud, fluid in the tires is useless because you sink down faster. You got too much weight. One turn of the wheel and you're on the axle. If you're light you can pull *through* mud a lot easier than if you're heavy. In the mud, if your tractor's heavy you'll drop a lot faster. Even pulling a load. I proved that with Hunter Thompson. He put oversized tires on his tractor, and he was going to fill them with fluid. I told him he better try it in the mud with a load of corn before he put the fluid in them. And he tried it. He went through where he wouldn't think of going through before. It even surprised him!"

The original general-use tractors, introduced around World War II in the North Country,[4] were the twenty-five-horsepower Fords like the one Willie now owns. These tractors are small and maneuverable, and when used with plows, disks, choppers, and wagons scaled to their size, they have adequate power. Since World War II, however, farm machinery has increased in scale by at least a factor of four. Modern tractors have eighty to one hundred horsepower, and often four-wheel drive. They also cost between $50,000 and $100,000. These huge, powerful tractors can pull machinery scaled to their potential power and speed. The increase in the scale of technology makes it possible to tend fields more quickly (so a farmer can work more land with a single-tractor setup) because the tractor is moving faster and covering more ground. These ratios of increased horsepower to increased production make sense from the standpoint of simple efficiency (ignoring the problems of soil compaction and the amount of fuel these units require) in the American Midwest, where fields are miles long, flat, and relatively rockless. In the North Country, however, the fields are fitted in between woods and rock outcroppings; they are irregularly shaped, hilly, and sometimes as small as three or four acres. Local agriculture includes farmers who have adopted the latest machinery and others who have maintained older and smaller-scale technology. Willie views the issue:

"The farmers want the bigger stuff, but they haven't got that good a ground to get onto—it's mucky. They're all right when they're planting, but when they go to take their crop off they're in mud. That's the way the seasons are around here. So they go bigger and bigger—eighty, a hundred horses; four-wheel drive. And the four-wheel drive drops into the mud just as easy as a two-wheel drive. And then they got to get something bigger to pull it out.

". . . We've got people here sticking with the equipment they had twenty years ago. They're getting their corn off in the fall where the rest of them are stuck in the mud. They go slower, but they're getting their corn off faster than those with the big equipment because they're not breaking down and getting stuck. Little two-row tow chopper—that's big enough. Forty-eighty-horsepower Allis-Chalmers [tractor] is big enough. But they see that their neighbor has a bigger tractor, and they've got to have one too. The ones that still use a little Ford, like I've got, take a ribbing—they say it's just something to go after the cows with. But they can get down in the pasture and get out, where with the big tractor they can't! If you work steady you can go half the speed of the big ones and still keep up. Bob Labor has no problems when he starts taking corn off. He gets his corn off and sets around and watches these other guys get stuck in the mud! He's still got his small, original equipment. And he takes off a lot of acreage, too! He ain't taking full loads. He's taking half loads, but he's getting it in. Other farmers think they've got to fill that box right up to the top and pile it—but that's the worse thing you can do. Be gentle with it, take your time, and you'll get there."

It isn't only the length of the season and the weight of the machines that sometimes makes the largest agricultural equipment difficult to use. The machinery is hard to maneuver around corners and obstacles. The unevenness of the fields makes a six- or eight-beam plow, or a similarly wide disk and chopper, work *through* rather than over and around the contours of the fields.[5] Rockiness compounds the problems. The huge tractors and self-propelled choppers pull powerfully enough to break heavy steel against rocks. (It is true that the equipment pulled by the larger tractors is made from heavier metal. The heavier machinery can be, and is, abused more easily, but it is also harder to fix when it does break.) Smaller equipment goes over rocks or stops the tractor. And the driver of the smaller equipment is closer to the ground and better able to see what lies ahead. Finally, with the smaller equipment, ecological practices such as contour farming are much easier, again because of the basic maneuverability of the equipment. Willie sees these issues from the vantage point of the individual who is called upon to fix the machines that inevitably break. He states:

"You take a five- or a six-beam plow—it isn't that useful around where it's stony. The time they're wasting backing up and tripping plows and things—if they took a three-beam or a four-beam they could be gone. With the bigger equipment they've got the idea they're going to get done sooner. And some of them do, if they have luck. And some of them get done later, because they don't have that luck. When they have a breakdown it's more expensive to fix. Plus they've got a lot bigger investment, and the way it's going now, a lot of them that went that way—they're the ones that are going under. They couldn't afford it. They overbought."

It is not that the farmers with larger equipment are less responsible than farmers with smaller equipment. Willie sees that as the farmers have evolved to equipment that is larger, more complex, and considerably more expensive, they have also moved further from *intimate* knowledge of the individual pieces of machinery they use. As Willie fixes a wheel harrow he talks about the kind of maintenance the smaller equipment engenders.

I begin by asking what caused clamps to loosen, leading to the breaking of a heavy brace that holds the disk.

Willie answers, "Stones, or just the working of the machine. When those disks hit a stone, it doesn't have to be a big one, it'll make it bounce. The jar of it stretches the metal. The wheels don't break—they're case-hardened steel. I've got some old ones up there I use under my floor jacks—my safety stands. Those are disks out of wheel harrows.

"A good farmer tightens those up every time he uses them. This farmer does. But if you're doing a ten- or fifteen-acre field—and most of his fields are anywhere from fifteen up to twenty—you try to get through one of them before you tighten up the disks and go to the next field. But sometimes it doesn't work that way. It depends on how many stones there are in that field. And when you're driving a tractor, watching where you're going, you don't always have your eyes on those wheel harrows when they hit that stone. So you don't know how many stones you've already hit.

"The older disk harrows were set up different, and they were smaller. They'd bounce over stones where these won't. These are made in a wider surface— one beam goes clear across. They don't work separately like the older ones did. The older ones would play more when they'd hit a rock. Now they've got the big tractors and they want the big wheel harrows, and this is what happens. I think these go up to a nineteen-inch wheel. They cut in deeper, but your other wheel harrows will cut in four, five inches, six—depends how heavy you want to set them. The older wheel harrows had bunks on top of them made out of angle [irons] where you could lay stones for weight, if you wanted to cut deeper. . . .

"A farmer would use a set of the older wheel harrows two, maybe three seasons before he would have to do any repair on them. They're repairing these [newer models] every season. There's always something going wrong with them. The old wheel harrows had grease fittings on the bearing blocks. The new ones— mostly they're dry blocks—dry bearings. Prepacked bearings.

"It's a good sturdy bearing, but it's prepacked and it doesn't take long if you're in the mud and dirt—the prepacking seal wears out, and the first thing you know you've got a bearing gone. Where on the older ones you go out everyday with the grease gun—you greased them, and you pushed the dirt out. In fact, most of them never had a seal on them. You just greased them and pushed the dirt out. But you were paying attention to it every day, and you could see if something was loosened up. I think people were more *alert* to things in those days, too. They knew what they had. This stuff is getting so technical, half of the farmers don't even know what they've got. If they want to know something about it they've got to go get the book to look it up."

Willie's values include the idea that machines ought to be scaled to local conditions. It follows that people should know their machines and monitor their wear and adaptation to changing conditions on the land. These values are ecological because they imply knowledge of nature and machines in changing relation to each other. The values reflect the desirability of a balance between the natural and the human-made that is least damaging to the natural while fulfilling human needs.

The ecological character of Willie's values is also shown in the way he uses the land and machines for his own livelihood. "Ecological" in this sense does not suggest suburban tidiness. I am speaking, for example, of how Willie harvested local materials to build his house. Although the materials are not all standard by modern building techniques, Willie adapted his designs to make them work. In fact his methods, based on adapting his construction techniques to the wood from his own land, resemble those of the first house builders in the area. (Our own farmhouse, dating from the 1860s, was built with wood from the trees cleared for the first fields. Much of the studding and rafters is mixed hardwood cut locally. The interior trim is made from the butternut and chestnut that once grew there in profusion.)

Willie sited his house to take advantage of southern exposure for solar gain. He is building a greenhouse to make the house largely energy self-sufficient and constructing a hot-water system from a salvaged gasoline storage tank. He is slowly accumulating batteries for an electrical system already designed to detail in his head. When my wife and I built an in-ground solar greenhouse Willie worked closely with us, suggesting design features and helping solve construction problems. By Willie's estimation our design was not radical enough—he would have sited the building so it could also heat the house and would have added several features that would, in his estimation, significantly increase the efficiency of the solar heating system.

Willie's designs are often deceptively simple, and they generally use readily available material. He designed a solar heating system for a neighbor's swimming pool that used cheap black plastic piping instead of copper pipe. The original system, adapted from a solar energy magazine, had not worked. Willie expressed his frustration when he explained how the man had refused to believe Willie could make a system that would work after the system designed by solar experts had not. Willie's system was less exotic and far cheaper, but it heated the swimming pool.

At the same time, many of Willie's designs do not get finished, or they are set back because he works alone not only building his inventions but generating the income needed for his whole operation and, at the same time, doing a substantial amount of work on many of his neighbors' similar problems. When he built his shop in the early 1970s, for example, he laid plastic pipe throughout the concrete floor to carry heated water. If the floor on the Quonset was warm, he reasoned, even if the air was chilly it would be possible to work in reasonable comfort. At that time oil was inexpensive, and Willie's system operated with an oil-fired hot-water heater. During the mid-seventies oil prices increased more than fivefold, and Willie designed a wood-fired boiler to replace the oil-burning system. It was also during this period that Willie was very ill in two years during the winter months. The shop was left unattended during a forty-below-zero cold spell, and the pipes in the floor of his shop froze and snapped. The setback meant the end of a good system; to fix the pipes the floor would have to be broken up with a jack-hammer. In the meantime the shop has been heated with wood furnaces—an adequate system, but not as good as the original. When these setbacks occur Willie adapts and carries on. Although the principles that guide his work remain the same, his disappointment at these setbacks is sometimes acute.

Because Willie lives close to natural processes, he understands them. Although he works primarily on machines, his understanding carries over to the natural settings where the machines are used. Human needs, technology, and the local environment thus continue to evolve in relation to each other.

Work and Self

A person is many things—mate, parent, worker, entertainer, community member. Self-consciousness, and sometimes self-deception, integrates the often contradictory demands of different roles. In traditional or preindustrial societies there are relatively few of these personal role contradictions. Willie's community, though tied to industrial society, is in this way a great deal like the traditional world. Work is the well from which the other components of self are drawn. The single source makes the different roles minor variations rather than entirely different personae. In the following I study Willie's sense of himself both in the immediate sphere of his work and in the context of his community.

Willie finds himself in his work. To study Willie's attitude toward work, then, is to study his attitudes toward his own being. This is best done in the family and community contexts in which the work exists.

Willie's children have grown up knowing their father, in large part, by helping him work. As I have watched Willie showing one of his children how to do a job, a sequence from *Nanook of the North*, a 1922 documentary of Eskimo life, has often come to mind. As Nanook teaches his young son to shoot his miniature bow and arrow at a tiny snow polar bear—patient, ever attentive, warming his son's hands with his own—the viewer is shown that the Eskimo experiences the world directly and that the skills needed to manage it are known by the father and taught to the children. Willie's children recognize his skill and understand its value because they see and participate in the work of the shop and overhear the conversations and stories that are always going on. Willie's skill is also relevant to their personal worlds—it is not only their bikes, their motor scooters, and eventually their automobiles and houses that Willie helps them assemble or maintain. One day I was a bit startled to find Willie bent over white lace fabric spread on the floor of his house, making a dress (without a pattern) for the confirmation ceremony of one of his daughters. The idea that his children know their father through his work seems simple. But it is unusual in a society where most fathers work away from home, doing things their children do not really know about and that are in any case probably irrelevant to the children's own needs or problems. Willie's authority as a parent, then, is related to his children's recognition of his skills and the frequent relevance of those skills to their own lives.[6]

His relationship with his wife is also strongly rooted in his work. In a number of ways the shop represents the collective work of a family. Pauline often helps with jobs, shares the paperwork or the hassles that go with collecting on bad checks, and feeds people who are in her house because of their business with Willie. Although the work is collective, the division of labor is based on traditional male and female roles. Willie often makes it clear that though many people participate in the work of the shop, he is—at the center—the provider.

Finally, Willie's self-image exists in the context of the community. His status, born in his work world, extends into such varied roles as candidate for the office of highway supervisor, president of his bowling league, organizer of citizens band radio activities, and leader in public hearings over zoning legislation.

Willie's self-image comes, then, from the various human contexts he lives in. It also comes from the self-consciousness that arises from his working experience. This self-recognition has several elements. Overall, Willie's accounts reflect an understanding of the effect good work has upon a person. He typically discounts, with no false modesty, the specialness of his talents, yet he also identifies his work as unique and important to the community. Finally, he recognizes and uses the social power that comes from having knowledge and skill needed by others.

Willie discounts his skill by suggesting that the key to his method is patience and the willingness to do jobs others will not take on. Many mechanics do not accept the jobs Willie does because they are too ill defined, too time consuming, and even, one can say, too difficult. The blower repair detailed earlier, for example, came to Willie because "nobody else would fix it." Willie discounted the particular difficulties of the job with the statement that all the job required was patience. This is a common theme Willie sometimes plays with. Recently, for example, a new customer brought him a water-pump casing with three bolts broken off even with the surface. Willie began with a frown: "*Oh-oh—cast* and steel—*that's* trouble!" The man told Willie he'd been to a machine shop in town, but they couldn't fix his pump. I envisioned a long process of drilling out the studs, extracting the pieces, and rethreading the holes. Willie clamped the casing in his vise, brought out a small punch he had sharpened on one side, and picked up a tiny ball peen hammer. He carefully turned the broken pieces out of the casing by hammering ever so delicately with the beveled punch on the uneven surface of the broken studs. But when the customer hailed his accomplishment, Willie replied that the other machinist could easily have done the job; he just didn't want to be bothered with such stuff. It may or may not have been true, but in any case it was a characteristic disclaimer.

Willie does, however, understand that his patience is unusual and important to his own working method. "Oh, yes," Willie once replied, "you get stumped. But you've got to be a little calm, a little patient, and figure out *why.*"

To succeed at repairs other mechanics either haven't wanted to attempt or could not manage certainly fosters a positive self-image. Part of Willie's satisfaction comes from his capacity, already discussed at length, to focus on each step of a task as equally important. And part of the satisfaction, one can assume, comes from the simple problem solving in his daily work. Willie put it this way:

"A lot of them that come in here are pretty impatient. If you rush through things, you can't enjoy them. And it's a challenge—no job's the same. If you had a thousand jobs in a year, not two of those thousand jobs would be the same. Even the ones that are supposed to be the same aren't. Things are broken or worn in different ways—they each have their own characteristics."

Although Willie often discounts his skill, he also recognizes its quality. He tells some stories over and over, such as how he established his reputation with

the owner of the local Saab dealership by fixing the first Saab transmission he'd ever seen in three hours less than shop time for the job. But usually when Willie tells these stories it is because he cannot believe others could not easily do as well. At times a story tells how he put an unusual material to use, such as when he made a head gasket for a tractor from a sheet of copper ("that was twenty years ago, and that tractor is still running—it's owned by the town of Louisville"), or relates his ability to save his customers money by solving their problems more simply than other mechanics thought possible.

Willie also sees himself as something of a visionary. He patiently explains his designs and their logic to customers and friends. It might be an electrical system, a solar heating design, or a novel approach to a mundane repair. If the listener cannot fully grasp what he is talking about, Willie approaches his subject from several directions until the listener is at least convinced that *Willie* knows what he is talking about. I once asked Willie when he had begun the designing and engineering that is now such an important part of his work. He told me about making a violin out of a cigar box as a school project for the county fair, winning twelve dollars and a blue ribbon. Then he pointed to a small wooden airplane that hung up by the ceiling, nearly hidden between the beams.

"That airplane was made back before many people thought airplanes should look that way. Everyone laughed at me when I was making it. A few years after that was made, airplanes started to look like that. They were all double wingers before that. I made that in 1936. . . . That took first prize in the fair, too. I whittled it out with a knife—every bit of it. I was just a boy. I used shoe nails—cobbler nails they call it—to put it together with. My father used to do all our shoe work."

We take the airplane down to examine it more closely. I comment that the joints are still tight.

"Lost the wheels off it—the landing gear—that got broke off. . . . My idea for that was out of Buck Rogers. I called it a Buck Rogers plane at the time. Your five-passenger planes came out looking like that. . . . I figured that was the safest place to hang it—up there out of sight! You start looking at that and you start reminiscing, though, about school days. I was about eleven years old when I carved that out—ten or eleven, something like that. And I was fifteen or sixteen when we made our first glider. Our gliders were built on the same principle as this. But we rode in those."

The engineering, embedded as it is in the daily work of the shop, cannot be separated from the continuing work of repair. Willie summed up his attitude toward his whole range of mechanical skills:

"It's like when I was taking aviation mechanics. The guy who taught us says, 'Some of you boys will go out of here mechanics, and some of you will go out of here as parts exchangers—you'll never be a mechanic.' It's a type of knowledge that you can pick up and store in your mind. Quite a difference between the two. And we've got more parts exchangers around here than we've got mechanics. Fewer people find out the reason something has broken and solve the problem as well as maybe changing the part."

Willie is, in his own eyes, a mechanic. That identity is reconfirmed every time a job is completed.

Willie also recognizes the importance of his work to the community, and this recognition contributes a significant part of his overall self-image. He knows he is good at what he does and that his work is often crucial to his neighbors. Although some of this work gets neighbors out of mechanical jams, the primary responsibility Willie expresses is to the farmers he works for. This responsibility is expressed indirectly toward the farmers and more directly toward their work. During the peak periods in the farmers' schedules Willie works long hours. It is not uncommon on a rainy day in the summer to find five or six farmers at the shop, waiting their turns as Willie fixes and mends others' equipment. This is one way he put his attitude toward this work:

"I've worked for the farmers around here for so long I can't turn them away. Their work comes ahead of anything else. A guy's broke down in the field— they've got to get fixed and get back working. Because weather has a lot to do with their work. I've been with these farmers twenty-seven years."

Perhaps the most telling example of his attitude toward work, and thus self, is his view of those his own age who live on disability payments. When I first began spending time at the shop I found the number of these men who stopped by or hung around to be surprisingly large. It appears to be a form of early retirement for many working-class men, some of whom look quite healthy. Many of the real health problems are the result of industrial accidents. Others are caused by diseases like arthritis, hypoglycemia, or, quite commonly, diabetes (called "sugar"). Willie himself suffers, often severely, from the effects of his industrial accident and from hypoglycemia, but he continues working. He spoke about the issue:

"You know the thing that gets me, though, on something like that—he's [a man who often came to the shop] more able to work than I am, and he's drawing disability. He claims he can't use his arms. *I* can't raise my one arm up and use it the way I'm supposed to, either. See, even when I scratch my head I use my other hand! [Scratches head.] Some of the ones on disability have lost it because they got sent to a different doctor when they went back to be reclassified, and the doctors found out there was nothing wrong with them. Some guys have artificial legs, or partial artificial legs—several of those. Some are wearing braces. I know guys that have worked every day of their lives who are that way."

I ask Willie why he didn't go on disability after his accident:

"They put me on [classified me as] full disability. I refused it, because I'd have to close the shop if I took it. With compensation disability—you don't work. You can't work at all, unless they give you percentage disability. If they'd given me percentage disability I'd be all right. But they gave me full disability."

"In the ten years I've known you," I say, "you've had a lot of illness that seems to be connected with that old injury."

"Oh, yeah. Like right now I'm hurting in my shoulder. And this arm is just like a toothache. I didn't take my pain pills like I'm supposed to. Which I forget quite often. Intentionally, most of the time."

The decision not to stop working to gain disability payments is perhaps most important because it signals Willie's view of the proper role of work in a person's life. It is true that the net of social services, because of his low income and frequent illness owing to his old injury, has extended to Willie and his family in the form of assistance for medical bills, occasional surplus food, and so forth. These are seen by Willie, and others in his environment, as legitimate claims from a working person temporarily in need of help.

The Moral Universe of Work

Willie explains his values through his stories. There is a great deal of this storytelling, enough that it forms a small tradition with familiar contours and themes.[7] The stories are a type of folklore that comes out of work experiences,[8] and as such they are a natural extension of his work. They reflect a sense of social mastery that matches his technical mastery.

The stories, like traditional folklore, are reasonably consistent. They are often retold, sometimes with variations. Through the retelling, however, the stories become a small oral tradition for customers and friends who frequent the shop.

Richard Dorson said that in this modern folklore we find "the direct reflection of the central anxieties, aspirations, and concerns of [a small corner of] the contemporary era" (1981, 2). For Willie these anxieties, aspirations, and concerns include managing one's personal affairs in a market arrangement (essentially a meeting of parties with opposing interests), dealing with unscrupulous associates, and handling issues that touch the bureaucratic institutions of modern life. The stories reflect the social concerns of working-class life,[9] and many of the themes resemble those found in working-class popular culture, particularly in the lyrics of country and western songs. These themes can be summarized as a belief in the need for personal action, often against bad odds, or the facelessness of a criminal justice system based on distant and bureaucratic procedures.[10]

Finally, Willie's stories are performances. They are well told and often seem to be part myth and part reality. Whether or not they are literally true in all details, they are enjoyable to hear. The storytelling slows the pace of work and keeps Willie the center of attention in the shop. They are understood by everyone as simplifications of the world that reflect the group's wishful thinking. Willie is a kind of hero, independent in a social universe where most people are not. He is sought after and respected; somewhere Willie always seems to have the ace he needs up his sleeve.

I've chosen the examples that follow from scores I've heard at the shop. The stories appear in the ebb and flow of work, in natural pauses Willie uses to pace himself. They were not tape-recorded because they generally do not appear outside the context of work. The stories require an audience, and they often elicit a similar story from one of the listeners.

Many of the stories show how animals help Willie through various schemes. Some of the allies are rather predictable:

"My younger brother and I used to take off on the weekends back into the hills. We'd leave Friday night and get back in time for school on Monday. We'd take a bow and arrow, maybe an ax. But you know, we'd never sleep on the ground. No *sir*! We'd either climb a tree and tie our belt around a branch or go into a cave and build a fire at the opening."

"Rattlers?"

"No, black panthers. Black mountain cats. We'd be up in that tree, and Rover'd stay right at the base. If a cat came by he'd wake us—not with barking, but with a low growl. The cat'd hear him and go around. We'd hear him and watch for the cat. Those cats go a hundred fifty pounds!

"One time a bear got after us. We were up in a tree sleeping, and all of a sudden the tree starts shaking. Hell, we were only eleven or twelve at the time. Rover was down at the creek getting a drink or something, and that damn bear's shaking the tree! See, you've got to be careful, if you get in too small a tree the bear can shake you out, and if you get in too big a tree he can climb up after you! So I started yelling for Rover. Finally he heard me, and he came running and yelping. He got behind that bear, and he'd get right in and get a nip out of his ass! Circle around him—just stay out of reach. Damn bear got madder and madder at that dog, and he finally got sick of chasing around in circles and he took off. There were two scared kids in that tree! Full moon—we watched him go.

"So and so would say to my dad, 'You let your boys run in those hills?'

"Well, I guess he did. He taught us how!"

Some of the allies are less ordinary:

"I came out the door one day and found a garter snake with a toad half in and half out of his mouth. I killed the snake and pried open the jaws to let the toad out. He just sat there—dazed like. See, the snake has poison he stuns 'em with. The toad had got some of that poison, but not enough to kill him. He just sat there, eyelids blinking real slow, for three or four hours. I brought him in the shop so no one would step on him. Finally, that night he got better and hopped away.

"The next day he was there by the door waiting. I moved him again so no one would step on him. And that was where he lived—right there near the door in that pile of iron. Four years he caught insects for me. There weren't hardly any insects left around here. Then finally one year he didn't show up. But at the end he was so fat—big as my fist—he could hardly move."

Another time Willie and I were in the woods, cutting large hemlock trees we would mill for lumber for my wife's greenhouse. It was late in the summer, and nut trees were ready to drop their fruit. Willie was making plans to gather some, and I asked how you keep the squirrels from getting them all. Willie replied:

"You work with 'em, not against 'em. You let the squirrels pick your nuts!" I waited for a few seconds to take the bait.

"Now, just how do you do that?"

Willie explained, with exaggerated patience: "You take a piece of sewer pipe, like the one you just bought for your drain system—only the squirrels like ceramic better than plastic—and put it down near the trunk of the tree, and the squirrels will fill 'em up. Butternuts, walnuts, even some chestnuts. All of 'em. Old Mickey wouldn't believe me; he wouldn't try it. So every year he'd try to pick his own nuts, and they'd all be gone. After a few years he tried my idea, and by Jesus, he had bushelsful! But he fucked up. I told him to leave some for the squirrels, but he had to get greedy and took 'em all. So the next year he tried it again, but it didn't work—the squirrels had all left!"

Many of the stories reflect Willie's view of his own social power in more typical settings. Willie paints himself as someone who keeps the upper hand by making sure his knowledge is not *too* freely spread around. You've got to ask for help, and he doesn't always bend over backward to supply it. Willie explained:

"In school once they were trying to take a differential apart. They were hammering and beating on it, hammering and beating. The shop teacher kept looking over at me—I was just standing back watching. Finally he comes over to me and says, 'How do you take that apart?' I said, 'Well, the first thing you've got to do is pull those three set studs that hold your bearing in the back.'—'*Set* studs?'—'Yeah, on the outside,' I said. 'You got three in there. And there's lock nuts on them. You take them—back them out. Next thing you do is take a *small* hammer, tap the end of them, instead of that sledge hammer. Hit the driveshaft.' He says, 'Why didn't you tell him that?' I said, 'No one asked me.' So he walked over and told them to take the set studs out. They took them out, and I stood there looking dumbfounded like I didn't know. He says: 'All right, take that little hammer I use and hit the end of that shaft.' One guy picks the little hammer up and he reefs her one—the shaft went clean across the floor out of it. He came over to me afterwards and says, 'You know, you could have told us. We spent a day and a half on beating on that—we couldn't get it apart.' I became his *assistant* after that."

Willie tells a similar story of his son's experience in the large shop where he works in a local town:

"When their service manager is gone, well, he's their service manager. He works, plus he takes work in. And when a car comes in he knows what's wrong with it, but he'll let the service manager try to figure it out. And usually the service manager is about 75 percent wrong. Skip won't go over and give his advice unless it's asked for. If the service manager comes out and tells him to do something—he does it, even though it's wrong. When the service manager treats him right he'll tell the service manager what's really wrong with the car. But he lets the service manager come to him."

Withholding or granting information is a powerful means of controlling relationships. Willie does it as a matter of course, yet it does not carry a mean-spirited intent. He does it to control his personal encounters—to quietly, in fact passively, steer face-to-face interactions. Skip has in the meantime been promoted to service manager in the garage where he works. The technique works well for both men.

In Willie's world, when you are placed in a situation where you cannot engineer the dynamics of personal interactions, you sometimes have to act dramatically. Many of his stories have the theme of taking the law into your own hands when people such as corrupt policemen threaten. Willie told the following story in response to a trucker's tale of being cheated by those who are supposed to embody the law:

"Cost me $4,465 last time I went through North Carolina—that was a *bad* trip!" the trucker says.

"That's a considerable amount of money," I say. "What the hell did you do?"

"Overweight, just overweight," he answers. 'State regulation is seventy-two ton, two hundred fifty. I was four ton over. They stuck me with the fine for the whole amount."

Willie interrupts: "They can't do that! You should have called the federal boys! That happened to a friend of mine. They pulled him over and pulled the same stunt. He got back into the truck, and when they weren't paying any attention he got her back on the highway. Oh, they came after him! Set up a roadblock at the state line, but he barreled right through—smashed the hell out of the two state cars that sat across the road. Soon as he got over the state line he stopped and called the feds. He told them what had happened, and they let him go. They can't do that—that's double taxing. The weight limit is for taxes, it's not for the road or anything else. If you're over you just got to pay for the extra, plus a fine—probably a couple hundred."

"I know," the trucker says, "but what can you do? They've got you by the balls! Got your truck, got your load."

"Ever drive through Chicago?" Willie asks by way of answering. "I drove a load of cabbages up to Chicago, nonstop from Florida. The load was timed; I had only enough ice in the reefer to get it there nonstop. But I got stopped outside Chicago, and they were fooling around with us. I show the cop the shipping order and say, 'You better get out of the way, mister!' They had us boxed in, a car in front and one behind. 'What are you going to do if we don't?' he asks. 'Wait and see,' I tell him. See, they can't keep you if you've got a load of perishables. We had to get those cabbages to the market, so by God I creamed his car and headed out. They pulled their guns—I could see them in the mirror—but my partner took out our sawed-off shotgun and stuck it out the window. They saw that, and we didn't hear anything from their guns. They followed us all the way into Chicago, sirens wailing and lights flashing. We pulled right into the market, pulled up to unload. The cops were waiting for us. And the militia—did you know they had a militia there? They were all there— caused quite a ruckus, but right through it all they were unloading that cabbage. My partner was so scared he was shaking. I was scared too. But when we told them what had happened—that we were being held up and we had to deliver on time—nothing happened to us. 'Who's going to pay for our car?' the state boys ask. The city cops—see, they don't get along so good with the state boys and the state boys were on their turf—said, 'If you'd had the sense to get out of the way, nothing would have happened to your car!'"

The trucker is put down, and maybe he doubts Willie's story just a little. He says he was trying to get his partner into conversation with the cops so he could walk away from the group, get to his rig, which was at the end of a line of trucks, and highball out of there. But he hadn't acted, though he knew he was being taken. Both he and Willie agreed that the money wasn't going to the state treasury—so Willie had no sympathy. The world is constantly testing you, and you're likely to get the shaft if you don't act decisively when the situation demands.

Although Willie's stories often include the idea that you have to act decisively, even violently, when circumstances are controlled by corrupt but powerful people, they more often show that you can win through cleverness. Somewhere along the line the people who are supposed to be the watchdogs of public morality will see your point and help you out. The theme appears many times, in different versions. The following account shows the typical contours:

"Thirty-years ago," Willie begins, "I was working in Maryland, right at the factory where they make the Cat dozers. A guy from the city comes in—he wanted a dozer blade just the width of the city sidewalks to use on their small Cat. He was talking to the man in the front, but he sent him back to me. I told him I could do it in a week. 'That soon?' he says, real surprised. It took five days. I disassembled it and rebuilt it from the ground up. It was no big thing, but the other company there stole the patent, and now they're made just like the way I designed them.

"And that wasn't the first time that happened. You know those road leveler trailer hitches? They've got a torsion bar in them hooked up to bring the rear end of the car up level when you're pulling a big travel trailer. They're standard fare now. Well, a guy and I were working in his garage behind his house. He needed something to keep the rear end of his car from dragging when he hauled his trailer. We tinkered. Put together this thing with the torsion bars. It was a good idea; we talked to a company about making them. Then ninety days later another company sued him, saying they had the patent rights. I knew we could beat it, but I didn't know how. I studied the photographs the company supplied of their hitch. It looked like the one my friend and I made, but I didn't remember anybody taking any photographs of his car. I got out the magnifying glass, and right in the bottom of one of the pictures was the license plate, his plate! So we went to court. For two hours we listened to the company talk about how they had been working on this thing for years. Finally I ask the judge, 'Do you mind if I say something?' 'Why *sure*, he says. 'Could I see those photographs again?' I say. I study them real carefully and say, 'That's Donny's car.' And oh, no! you should have heard them deny that. So I took out my magnifying glass, and I read off the numbers in the license plate. The judge asks Donny the numbers of his plate. 'Just a minute,' he says, as he pulls his registration out of his pocket, and then he reads off the numbers. Stopped them cold. Well Donny countersued, and he won. The company had to buy the rights to build them, and they had to pay him a royalty on every one they made. Donny kept the patent. I don't know how much he got out of it, but it was considerable."

The adversaries need not be remote companies. In the following account neighbors, who should know how to live in the community, take advantage when they have a chance:

"I used to use dynamite when I was drilling wells," Willie begins. "I was forty-five feet down once, through eighteen feet of bedrock, and we hit a big rock. The drill kept going off to the side. You can't force your way around a rock; it'll bend the casing, and you'll be stuck. So we pulled the casing up three or four feet, and I measured down the exact depth of the hole. I lowered a bundle of sticks down in there and let her go. That took care of that rock! But a funny thing happened on that job. It was over on the Norfolk road, and the Benji brothers that are drilling just down our road now were over there working. I made an arrangement with Joe to rebuild an old drilling rig for them—to get it into running condition so they could trade it in on a new rig—and for that work I got the use of the machine on the well I was going to drill. I was to buy my casing from them. So I got ready to drill; got the machine all fixed and ready to go. I got old Art Hunter to find the water on the land. But I cut the willow rod. He was going round and round in circles; finally up on the hill he says, 'Here it is.' I says, 'OK, if that's all you can find, but I want it down in the hollow.' I put a rock on the spot he marked. He comes down and circles round in a smaller and smaller pattern. Finally he finds it. 'Mark it here,' he tells me. Then I measured the distance between the two rocks. 'Why are you doing that?' he asks me. The distance was fifty-seven feet between the two rocks, and do you know, it was fifty-seven feet down to where we struck water? I don't know how I knew; I just knew. But then I started drilling, and I got that well down there fine once I got that rock out of the way. I cut the casing off four feet underground, like I was supposed to, and one day when I wasn't there one of the brothers came by and picked up the extra pipe. I had paid for seventy feet. I let it go. Then a couple of months later I got a bill for $300 from the other brother. I went right over: 'What the hell is *this*?' 'You got to pay for the use of the machine whether we were there or not,' he says. 'It's just the same whether we're there or not.' I told him about the arrangement I had made with his brother. He didn't care; he told me he was going to collect. By God, he sued. We go to court, and the judge asks me, 'Why didn't you make good on this bill?' 'That wasn't the arrangement we made, Your Honor.' I had three witnesses who were there when the deal was made. The machine I had fixed had been traded already. When their attorney heard what I had to say—I didn't have an attorney myself—he said, 'How about we just drop this?' The judge asked me if that was all right, and I said, 'Hell no! What about that pipe they took from me that I paid for?' That pipe was seven dollars a foot; that was twenty years ago, and I had had to go to the bank for that money. I wasn't about to let that go. The judge asks me what I figured they owed me; I figured it up and told them. Their attorney started to balk, and I told them to go to hell; I'd countersue. Finally I got the pipe back; I've used pieces of it in the shop there for years. I nearly countersued anyway for harassment, and do you know that to this day those sons of bitches won't talk to me?"

Willie's stories tell of his ability to control relationships with most of the people and institutions he deals with. I think that his interpersonal confidence comes from his mechanical mastery. The group he lives among sees him as, to put it simply, one of those in control. The less powerful, however, also tell stories about how they take on the world. These are often told in response to a story by Willie, in a verbal give-and-take. For the unemployed, those working in dead-end jobs in a depressed rural area, or those waiting out years of disability, the moral fables have the opposite relation to their worlds. They create a fiction that contrasts with their lives, or they interpret the tellers' experiences to show how, despite appearances, they are among the winners in life. The following story represents this general category of story well. The speaker is an unemployed former janitor, a "regular" at the shop. Eddie is unhandy and relies on Willie to keep many of his old and deteriorating machines in running order. Eddie comes almost daily and often brings little more than his stories. His stories, however, are given the same attention as the tales of any of those who use the shop as an audience for their moral fables:

"I worked up at a school in Massena," Eddie begins. "I used to get along with the kids pretty well. The other janitor was a mean one and the kids would get to him by throwing rocks through the windows, but it'd be me who'd have to fix them. Up that sixteen-foot ladder—ten below—putting those big pieces of glass in. That was in the beginning.

"I'd go in on Saturday morning. I didn't have to, but that'd make my week easier if I did—and one time some of those kids said, "Eddie, could we come in there and play basketball in the gym on Saturday morning?'

"I said, 'Sure, but I don't want you to go fighting or busting things up, and then when I'm about ready to go—about ten minutes before I go—I want you to take that big push broom out and clean off the floor.'

"Well, that worked out fine. Then I started letting them in in the morning too. I was supposed to let them in at ten to nine. They'd come early—or some of the buses had double runs and they'd be standing out there—some of them half-dressed when it was ten below zero. So I'd let 'em in and tell 'em to go down to the gym to play basketball or volleyball or to dribble around, you know—just use up some of that energy.

"Pretty soon the teachers started complaining. Course they had their own door and didn't have to stand out in the cold. But they started complaining that I was letting the kids in. My boss, the mean one, called me in and he says, 'Eddie, the teachers are getting down on me because you're letting the kids in!'

"I told him, 'By God I do let those kids in, and if you don't like it you find somebody else to run your school! You don't find any more of those windows broken, do you?

"'No, I don't,' he says; then things kind of quieted down. No more complaints for a while. But I found out who was complaining—my own neighbor. Short, fat woman. Taught third grade. She's say, 'Mr. Larson'—she didn't call me Eddie—'Mr. Larson, could you adjust my clock? I think it's one minute off!'

"Up to that third floor, lugging that ladder. But I got back at her too. The teachers had their own parking lot, but they'd leave their keys in, and if they were going to plow it out, well, I'd go and move those cars. Then on the real cold days I'd go out about ten minutes before they left and start their cars. Put the heater and the defroster on. They liked that! But you know I never got to her car. After about a month she comes by and says, 'Mr. Larson, do you think you'd have time to start *my* car?'

"'Nope,' I says, 'I don't think so!' And do you know, pretty soon there wasn't no more complaining, and there wasn't no more clock adjustment?"

The stories function in several ways. For many they make the relative powerlessness of modern working-class life more bearable. They certainly create, for tellers and listeners alike, a sense of belonging to a group that shares a working-class identity. For Willie the stories are consistent with his recognized status as one who, despite often considerable odds, works his way through mazes others can only wonder at. Willie's self-confidence is beyond question, and for many, I think, rather inspiring.

The stories that deal with the world outside the local community often have a different character. This may be because they reflect a reality that is not manageable in the same way one handles a face-to-face world. Bureaucracies are the impersonal organizations you sometimes have to borrow money from, or they may be the agencies of government that regulate your work or levy taxes. Dealing with bureaucracies often means coming to grips with circumstances that cannot be handled by logic, cleverness, or faith in a higher justice. Some are seen as serving honorable ends and are held in unusual respect. Others are seen as a necessary evil or are viewed as unnecessary and the work of bumbling people far removed from the realities of life. Still others are understood as quicksand that draws a person in and suffocates him. The important thread that connects all these attitudes is the idea that bureaucracies are not *of* the community (though they may be situated there); you cannot deal with a bureaucracy as you deal with those you live among. People are flexible, and while the final form of justice is firm and solid, the paths to it are circuitous. It is best to avoid the kinds of relationships a person has with bureaucracies, because they tend to lock people into an inflexible regime and punish them severely for erring. These ideas are illustrated in the following incidents and stories:

Willie was heading for Art Thompson's house to help him take down the chimney attached to his house trailer. Thompson was giving Willie the blocks as part of the payment on a bill for rebuilding his pickup. The chimney was coming down because the finance company was going to repossess the trailer on the following Tuesday. Thompson got on with people generally, but his work was of mediocre quality and the economy simply didn't support mediocre carpenters very well. He worked sporadically, but after six years of payments he'd fallen so far behind he couldn't make up the arrears. He and his wife would move into his garage, which he was turning into a house. A picture window Art had salvaged from a carpentry job was being framed in to replace the double doors. Footings were being poured for what he hoped would be an additional room. He had a drilled well and a septic system that would be adapted to the new building. I said it was a hell of a deal to lose your goddamned *house*. Willie simply said that was what happened when you bit off more than you could chew.

In another example:

Don, an unemployed man in his late thirties, was talking to Willie and me: "One time I bought a new truck. Never again. I was out west, making ten dollars an hour working as a welder. Bought me a new four-wheel-drive pickup—cost me ten thousand."

"You're a fool," Willie says.

"Had it a few months and the camshaft went out of it. Took it back to Chevrolet—it was a thousand miles over warranty, and they wouldn't fix it. So I says, 'OK, I'll pay to get it fixed, but I can't make the payments and fix it at the same time—let me skip a couple of payments and tack them onto the end.' 'Fine,' they said. The repair went over four hundred, so I missed two payments—they came and took the truck. Put it up for sheriff's auction and sold it for less than I still owed, so they put a lien on my wages to make up the difference. I'd put my old pickup for a down payment and I had to drive a lot for my job, so I lost that too. Then a year and a half later Chevrolet had a recall of all those engines—the camshafts were made out of bad metal and they replaced them all. By then the truck was long gone—no way to get it back."

"What did they say when they came for the truck?" I asked. "I thought you had an agreement."

"They didn't say nothing," Don answered. "They just took the truck. But I'll tell you—that was the last time I ever bought a new truck!"

"There never should have been a first time," Willie said.

You "put your name on the line" to get a machine that ought to make your life more simple, or pleasant, or manageable. But you can get caught and lose everything—truck, old truck, job, way of getting another job, house. On one hand Willie's lack of sympathy comes from his understanding that these purchases were merely beyond the means of his friends. On the other hand, the bureaucracies involved operate by a code quite different from a situation in which purchase and payment are a part of regular community give-and-take. This is not to say that lack of payment is less serious in Willie's world, but rather that the sanctions that enforce payment tend to be informal rather than formal. It is true that as the amount of money involved increases, the expectation that payment will be made in a regular fashion increases as well. But for someone who lives in the community—someone known, someone reliable, though not always *extremely* reliable—even exchanges involving large sums of money can be very informal. They would include the understanding that a person in a position of advantage may easily become the one at a disadvantage. Certain values are more important than specific procedures. Taking away a person's means of subsistence because of a late payment, for example, is committing a greater harm for a lesser gain. At the same time Willie, like many small entrepreneurs in similar settings, is not in as many relationships with bureaucratic organizations as are businesses in more prosperous areas. As creditors such small businessmen have less pressure and are intrinsically more flexible. When they must deal with strictly contractual relationships in which the punishment for mistakes is severe and unbending, they do so with the wariness of a mouse dealing with an owl. Most people who feel they have been burned avoid similar entanglements in the future. Don's response is passivity, a kind of general resignation that the world isn't too nice to deal with. Willie stays away from most involvements that are not face to face, and when he is forced to deal with organizations and contracts he does so very carefully.

Work and Community

On a night in early April we are in the midst of a particularly nasty late winter storm. The temperature is ten degrees and dropping. An unusual wind—forty miles an hour from due north—is driving the smoke back down the chimney of the greenhouse wood stove, filling the building with smoke and cold air. The greenhouse is full of small, vulnerable plants—most of Sue's spring crop of flower and vegetable seedlings. Attempts to get the fire burning hot enough to reverse the air flow fail. Finally Sue douses the fire with water and clears out the smoke with exhaust fans, lowering the temperature even farther.

We plug in two electric heaters, but they blow a fuse. The greenhouse is wired off three outbuildings, all with old entrance boxes and sometimes improvised wiring schemes. I cannot find the blown fuse in the system, have no electrical tester, and quickly come to the end of my knowledge. The wind blows unabated, and the temperature continues to drop. We feel a certain desperation, for this is the kind of problem in rural living that has no clear solution but simply must be solved. There are plenty of reasons to give up—the cold, the inconvenience, the subtlety of the problem. It is a situation farmers face again and again. In this case a year's crop will be lost if the greenhouse cools below freezing. The problem seems deceptively simple; air is going in the wrong direction down a chimney pipe. Considered more fundamentally, the issue becomes matching the performance of a machine to natural elements doing unusual things. Both the machine and the natural elements must be understood in enough depth to permit the proper adaptation and redesign. It calls for a kind of knowledge not found indexed in the yellow pages with clear hourly rates.

I call Willie. At first he chides me for not being able to get myself out of the fix I'm in, then he tries to instruct me over the telephone on how to proceed. He is surprised—as I was—that a hot paper fire won't reverse the air flow. He agrees to come.

We have called as friends who are also customers, but exactly what is meant by the terms "friends" and "customers" is not obvious. This is one of those times you cash in your chips. No one chooses to go out into the night in a winter storm on a job that may take hours. We would pay whatever was needed (or perhaps whatever an expert would charge), but Willie comes or does not come out of expectations that have built up over the years. It would be an insult—and would not work—to offer an exorbitant amount of money. And I know that if Willie comes he will come to solve the problem, not to give it a good effort and then leave.

It is half an hour before he arrives because he's had to make a circuit tester. He lent his to someone but can't recall who. Julie, age seven, has come along, though she is already dozing when they arrive.

We use the circuit tester in the barn, milk house, and cold frame to determine where the electricity has stopped. Finding the line dead beyond the milk house, Willie rearranges the four 250-volt two-inch cylindrical fuses in the box, isolating the one that has blown. There are enough good fuses to activate the side of the box that leads to the greenhouse. He tests the box by taking it apart and putting the bare ends of the homemade tester directly into the fuse contacts. The brilliant glare of the bulb on the tester is the first sign of success—and it brings comfort.

The air still blows down the chimney, bringing a yet deeper chill. Willie starts a paper fire, as we had done, to heat the pipe and establish an upward draft, but the smoke billows out of the stove around the door seal and damper, unable to match the force of the wind. Willie says that success depends on heating the pipe enough to pull the air upward—that the wind, no matter how strong, cannot reverse the flow of smoke once it is established.

The stove in the greenhouse is designed to move heated air from the stove into heat storage bins in the walls of the greenhouse. A fan blowing through a three-foot length of pipe forces air into the jacket built into the stove, then through small pipes into the storage bins. Willie removes the fan and blower, cradles the fan on his lap, and positions the end of the pipe tightly against the door of the stove so that air blows in through the damper holes. The fan forces the flames and smoke up the chimney, and the blast of air produces a quick, hot fire. We start three or four fires in this manner by putting papers in the stove, quickly lighting the fire, closing the door, and placing the fan assembly against the door to blow through the damper holes into the fire. Each time the process works for a moment. The heat, pushed by the fan, forces it way up the chimney, and the frost line on the chimney pipe moves upward. But then, as the fire dies, the flow of air reverses and the smoke again flows into the greenhouse. Each time the frost line moves back down the chimney, I feel as though we are battling the wind itself.

After the fourth or fifth try Willie says we will have to extend the chimney a few inches on the windward side. I have no sense for how much extension is necessary, thinking we'll need a lot more than a few inches to make any difference in the howling wind. I seek dramatic solutions and am impatient with slow progress. Willie and Sue make a ten-inch chimney extender, and I climb up on the roof to remove the spark arrester and install our improvised part. Then we begin again by lighting small fires, perfecting our method by mixing cedar kindling with the paper to make the fire last a bit longer, adjusting the damper to allow less air to enter the stove as we gain on the wind. As each fire dies, the wind gains back the pipe and the process begins again.

I become less discouraged when Willie notes that the front line is coming down a bit less each time and that the fires are lasting a little longer. Finally we light a fire with enough wood to continue on its own, and then with the fan removed from the front of the stove the final confrontation takes place—the wind puffs a few times through the leaks around the door and the damper but then gives way to the draft of the fire. As with many problems I've watched Willie solve, there are no quick and easy solutions, rather a series of slow steps modified along the way to a final solution.

We talk for an hour in the house, over coffee. Julie is asleep sitting up, at one in the morning. Willie makes ready to leave and I ask what I owe. He says simply "No," and it is left at that.

Values can be thought of as radiating in layers from the self. There are values that are the most private and basic, that give a person identity and guide personal action. Personal action engages with other "lines of action," formal or informal patterns of association in work and community, through a fitting together of several individual sets of values and beliefs. This fitting together, however, cannot be taken for granted, for it is an ongoing process, often fraught with conflict.

In a general way I am referring to the social interaction in the small, informal group. This interaction in Willie's shop is guided by informal expectations, values, and traditions that are part of both Willie's personal world and the mores of the community he lives in.

There are two aspects of the relationship between the shop and the community that can be simply expressed as word and deed. There are the stories, some of which I have already related, that are almost continually told in the shop—about good and bad deals, about getting even, about getting the upper hand. The stories carry the dual themes of instructing the listener on the proper way of acting and showing the teller—Willie—like the trickster, winning against difficult odds.

The other aspect of the relationship between shop and community concerns the nature of social interaction itself. Most of this book has been concerned with such issues, if only as a backdrop. I will now look at this more directly and add examples that show how the occasional bad deals are sorted into the daily working of the shop.

THE SHOP AS A SOCIAL SYSTEM

In general, everyone who deals at Willie's shop is quickly known if they have not been known before. People come for Willie's services because they have heard about his skill from others; there is no advertising, and the location is isolated.

The explicitness of the contract between Willie and a customer usually increases with geographic distance. Many who pull in to have their Saabs fixed pay an hourly rate (one-fifth of that charged by a Saab garage in a major city) for roughly the hours the Saab manual suggests a job should take. But for every job completed for amounts established by Saab shop manuals, many more are done as part of an intricate network that includes barter, the exchange of goodwill, loans of equipment, and participation in the sociability of the shop.

From another perspective, Willie's shop is the center of a circle of dependence that extends outward for eight or ten miles. Not everyone, of course, deals with or depends upon Willie. Among those who do are the very poor, who depend on makeshift machines. Yet the isolated rural area, coupled with the harsh environment, is a great equalizer. All share the common difficulty imposed by the weather and the isolation, and even those who are well off often depend on machines that are obsolete or worn out.

The relationships between Willie and his neighbors extend over years, decades, or whole lives, and when someone errs or takes advantage it is not easily forgotten. The social fabric, once torn, can sometimes be repaired. Willie will have the upper hand because his skills are in demand, but he may also be at a disadvantage because, for example, payment is often based on an informal agreement. When vulnerable, Willie may be taken advantage of; this in turn influences the next round when the person who has taken advantage is again in need of Willie's skills. What has been done cannot be undone, and people are often remarkably shortsighted about the future effect of their actions. Many of the people who take advantage do so because their poverty has forced upon them a certain desperation. Generosity and flexibility are easier when one is not scrambling to stay afloat. Willie sees this because he has experienced poverty, and he is often more forgiving than I would think reasonable. On the other hand, there are things a person can do that are not easily forgiven.

The following vignettes are examples of exchanges that are among the more problematic of those I have observed over the years. The emphasis here is on renegotiated order—the way the web of affiliation is rent or maintained in what are not unusual day-to-day circumstances.

Borrowing a Backhoe

It was late in the evening when Hunter McPherson stopped by to pay for a welding job completed the day before. Since most of the neighboring farmers have running accounts, it was unusual for someone to stop specifically to pay for an individual job. McPherson came and left quickly, and Willie was decidedly aloof and distant. In fact, when the man came through the door Willie went on working as though no one was there. Finally a nervous McPherson (twenty years Willie's junior) handed Willie a check, tried hard for some light talk, and fell over himself praising the job Willie had done. When Willie returned none of the conversation, he turned and left. I said, "You're a friendly bastard tonight!" Willie put down his tools. "Remember that backhoe we borrowed that we had to fix *and* pay for? Well, that's who we got it from!"

The year before, Willie had borrowed a tractor and backhoe from McPherson to dig a hole for the two-thousand-gallon solar heating tank he was installing in his front yard. Willie had dealt with McPherson's father for years, and the accounts often ran through a season. When it came time to borrow the backhoe, the understanding was that it was a loan, one of the things exchanged for the small favors Willie routinely extended to McPherson.

As Willie and Skip began the job, something broke inside the machine. The part had simply worn out, and it was Willie's misfortune to be using it at the time. But there was no question about fixing it—if you borrowed something and it broke while you had it, you fixed it whether it was your fault or not. Skip took two of his vacation days because the job required two men; the machine was torn down and a new hydraulic cylinder, which was quite expensive, was purchased and installed. Jobs in the shop were left, and new work piled up. As Willie and Skip installed the cylinder, they also completed several smaller repairs on the backhoe and tractor.

Thus Willie returned the machine in far better shape than it had been in when he picked it up. Young McPherson, however, informed Willie that *renting* him the backhoe had canceled the $400 debt their farm owed him. Willie didn't argue. Nothing could be done because the system was based on mutual understanding rather than formal agreement. Young McPherson had the momentary upper hand, and he used it to his advantage. He hadn't run the operation for that many years and perhaps thought his father's method was antiquated—that you could hustle and get ahead by manipulating traditional arrangements between neighbors.

Then McPherson didn't come to the shop for months; word was that he was taking his welding and farm repairs elsewhere. Finally he broke something that no one else could fix. He brought it in and Willie said he'd fix it, but for him all repairs were to be paid for when they were picked up. When he came for the machine the day before, he'd forgotten his checkbook; Willie told him to come back the next day. After he left Willie said, "He says my work is high—it is, for him. I told him to take it somewhere else if he didn't like my prices, but nobody else would do his work. So he's back, and I get him a little each time. He screwed me and he'll get it back—double."

This seemed like open declaration of war, yet within a few months things were back to normal. McPherson had mellowed somewhat from the experience and had again become a regular customer. The incident was mentioned only in passing and was treated with more humor than anger. In fact, within a few years it had become a distant backdrop. McPherson brought his machines, Willie fixed them, and we all bowled together on Wednesday nights.

When I asked Willie about the incident some years later, he remarked that there were times when people needed a little educating, but that you've got to live with your neighbors, so you've got to be patient with them too. There is no doubt that Willie's years-long relationship with the father influenced the way things were eventually worked out. Yet McPherson's act had been sorted into the ongoing events of the shop; for a time he paid a high price for his repairs, and his attitude of deference suggested he knew he had erred.

Floating a Tank and Fixing a Furnace

The kind of "sorting out" that happens in the routine of the shop goes on for years, between people who have known Willie in changing circumstances. Even those who are among the best known and liked sometimes inadvertently err:

Willie had known Pat O'Brien since he was a kid. There was great affection between the two men, but it was understated—left in the background. O'Brien had much of Willie's cleverness and stamina for a difficult job, but he lacked some of Willie's finesse and knowledge. Thus O'Brien was a common fixture at the shop, seeking advice, borrowing tools, using work space for his projects.

O'Brien's wife was from a nearby city. Their first house was a trailer, which she kept spick-and-span. People with dirty feet were supposed to remove their shoes. Willie, however, didn't take off his shoes for anybody; he stopped being a visitor in his old friend's new life.

As Willie and I were working on my septic system one day, he asked me if I knew how to get an old tank out of the ground. I imagined days of digging.

"That's what O'Brien thought. He moved into his first trailer over on the Norfolk road. He was putting in a new septic system; worked for two days with a back-hoe trying to get the tank out. He had dug all around it, under it, was working with chains trying to yank it out of the ground. Finally he called me. I said, 'You got water there, hose?' 'Why, *yes* I do.' 'I'll be over.' I hooked up the hose, started running water into the hole, sat back and lit a cigarette. He's bending over looking, still can't figure out what I'm doing. 'Better watch out,' I says, 'those things jump right out of there when they let go!' See, you float 'em out. Well, he thought that was pretty good; she came out of the ground just as nice as you please. After we got it out we were going into the trailer to get a cup of coffee, and his wife starts in about this taking off your shoes bit. I just turned around and left.

"I didn't see O'Brien for quite some time. Then one night it was down to forty below and his furnace quit. He couldn't figure it out—it was one of those jobs where the gun twirls around shooting the oil through the chamber. They don't make them anymore. He called me up about midnight, got me out of bed. Oh, I was nice and warm! I said, 'I'd come, but I wouldn't have much luck fixing it from the outside!' 'What do you mean?' he says. 'Well, if I got to take my shoes off I'm not coming inside.' Well, you should have heard him going at his wife. I could hear him over the phone. He says to me, 'Is that why you have been staying away?' Well we fixed that furnace, and we made a mess too. The whole thing was clogged with soot. But when I got there they were all huddled up with blankets, and when I left that furnace was going full blast. That was the last time she told me to take my shoes off. She got over that—now it's 'Well, come right in,' just like it is in my house."

Killing a Dog

There are things one can do, however, that take a person permanently out of the circle of the shop. This can be illustrated with an incident that included Robert Graves, a farmer in his mid-sixties whom I know as a neighbor but had never seen at the shop.

I had been working with Graves for a few days during the sugaring season. The second day out we found that the sap from the night before had run through the evaporator onto the coals of the fire. The evaporator is a four-by-eight-foot copper tray with three-inch grooves running from end to end, mounted above the chamber in which the wood fire blazes; sap is poured into the tray and boiled until the proper consistency of syrup is achieved. With age and use the copper deteriorates, particularly where it is in the greatest contact with the fire. Graves had broken small holes through the bottom of the grooves by cleaning them too vigorously; Willie later told me it is better not to clean the grooves at all, since residue from the boiled sap forms a glue that protects the thin copper. A new tray would cost upward of $2,000, and it would take time away from the best sap run to drive to Vermont to get one. The loss of days of sap in the middle of the short sugaring season and the expense of a new tray would be serious setbacks. Graves, generally an optimistic and cheerful man, was more upset than I'd ever seen him when we found the dry evaporator. I suggested we take the tray to Willie; it was just the kind of job he could usually work some magic on. Graves at first seemed unenthusiastic. I didn't push it but mentioned Willie's skills and his typical commitment to getting a farmer back to work, then he agreed that perhaps taking the tray to Willie's would be the best solution.

We disassembled the unit, loaded it onto the wagon, and hauled it out of the woods. The tray was awkward and heavy, and the job took a couple of hard hours. We took the tray to Willie's in the back of a pickup, and I was surprised to find a strange coldness when we arrived. I tried to start up the typical small talk that passed between us on most meetings, but my words brought no response whatever. Willie looked briefly at the overturned tray and said that a repair was impossible. There were many tiny holes, and the copper was so thin that heat sufficient to bond new material would melt more holes. The only real solution would be to begin replating where the leaks were worst and work along to the better metal. But as he examined the long grooves he said there really wasn't any better metal farther up the tray; there was no way to make it right. He turned to walk away. I pushed a bit—as I had never done before. I couldn't remember a time Willie hadn't at least tried a repair, especially to get an agricultural operation back to work.

When I prodded Willie assented; he silently gathered his tools and bent to the task. The braising required the most delicate touch. Too much heat would make a hole even larger. He had to feed the melted solder into the small holes that he had made just hot enough to accept the new metal. He worked without pausing for half an hour; when he straightened up for the first time he was finished. He said he wouldn't guarantee anything, but that the repair was as good as could be done. He named a price in an unusually direct manner, which wasn't cheap, and when payment was made he returned to work without the normal pause for a story. We wrestled the heavy, cumbersome, and yet delicate tray back into the woods and were elated to find that the repair had been successful. Three seasons later the tray is still boiling sap.

Six months later Willie and I were finishing a job together at two in the morning. We were exhausted, but Willie kept us going with tales of Sam, the super-dog. Of all the dogs he'd owned, Sam was his favorite, and stories about him were never in short supply. After a long story about how he'd taught Sam to eat onions, I asked Willie what ever happened to the dog. "It was your neighbor," he said. "Your neighbor shot him. Twenty years ago. Graves had a collie in heat, and Sam kept breaking out and trying to get to her. Even broke his chain. I told Graves to keep his dog in until she was through heat—how in hell are you going to keep the male away? Well, one day he shot Sam—the neighbor saw him and came and told me. We went looking for that dog, and we went right up to the house—oh no! they hadn't seen him. Well, that was the last time he brought his equipment here to fix! I wouldn't have fixed that evaporator of his if you hadn't brought him."

So I had unwittingly compromised Willie's code. Graves is a kind and honorable man. In fact, it was never established that he *did* kill the dog; it is just as likely that someone else killed it or that it was killed on the road. But Willie believed that Graves had killed the dog and acted accordingly. It was an act that was sorted into the system of exchange lasting years and years in a neighborhood close in miles but distant in social worlds.

Cutting on Shares

Even those who are "regulars," who have known Willie for years and are among his closest friends and most frequent customers, sometimes carry out their ends of deals badly. Their reintegration into the shop is seldom easy, though almost always possible.

It's a hard day at Willie's. There's no greeting, no joking around. I stay out of verbal distance, working on my own project. It's late October but beautifully warm and dry. The fall has been unusually kind, but now the days before winter are very few, and soon any projects left undone will be covered with mud and snow.

The sound of two chain saws cutting hurriedly, working fast, drifts to the shop. Bill Black and Tommy Mullen are in Willie's woods, cutting and drawing their wood for the winter. They're supposed to be cutting on shares, cutting and hauling as much for Willie as they take for themselves. But Mullen has taken three truckloads past the shop, each with four face cords, and brought none to Willie. Black has done little better—he's hauled for three days and brought only one pickup load for Willie. It hurts to hear those chain saws, because it drives home how much wood will soon be needed and how little time there is at the moment to be in the woods getting it. Several times Willie remarks to me, "That is the last time—that's the last time they get into my woods." But what, I say to myself, about this year?

The two men, both friends of Willie's for years, work all week. Ten days later I'm having dinner with Willie and Pauline when Mullen walks into the house without a knock. "Got any chain saw gas for me to use tomorrow?" he asks Willie. "Yeah, there ought to be some there," Willie answers. After he leaves I say, "I'm surprised to see Mullen. I thought you weren't going to let him back into your woods."

"He's going in for me," Willie answers. "Didn't you hear him in the bowling alley last week? We were over in the corner and he tells me, 'You ought to get your wood out—it's dry in there!' I just said, 'With two men working in my woods I shouldn't have to go in there at all.' He didn't say nothing—he just walked away. I said to hell with him. But you know, I can't stay mad at that son of a bitch—he's like one of my sons. I knew he'd be back."

I suspect that the deal about the wood had been more implicit than explicit. It is almost a custom—if you cut in someone's woods you give half to the owner. But it is an understanding that has to be enforced; it doesn't exist in the abstract. I don't think that Mullen or Black felt the pressure as a moral issue, a question of right or wrong. Rather I think they were being pragmatic—they needed the wood but didn't want to use up their welcome at Willie's. In this case it meant being able to call on Willie's services, Willie's wood, but more important, I would guess, it meant continued acceptance as part of the group formed at the center by the shop.

The next day a single chain saw rasped in the woods. Willie wasn't around. I walked to the woods to find Mullen blocking up two large ash trees he'd felled. He would bring his splitter and break up the chunks in the woods, and Willie could haul them out himself. As it turned out, the blocks were too long for Willie's stove and had to be cut in half. Mullen blew a hose on his splitter and didn't get it fixed before the fall rains and snow made it impossible to get into the woods with his truck. Willie wouldn't get what he said he deserved, but Mullen had done enough to get back into his good graces. At least he thought it was fair and said so. Black's contribution was less impressive. He gave Willie an overhead garage door. He was to install the door in the back of Willie's shop, but when they started the job Black made several mistakes; they had an argument, and he left. Willie did over what Black had begun and installed the door himself. I am sure that Black, too, felt he'd paid his dues, but the issue was difficult to figure: What is the worth of a salvage garage door poorly installed? What is the worth of Willie's standing wood, particularly if the supply is going to run short a few years down the line? What is the value of time spent in the woods in the dead of winter at work that would have been unnecessary had the shares been contributed?

All three of the men have limited resources, and the exchanges are rough and inexact; their fairness is hard to determine from the outside. It seemed that the exchange operated so that each party received and gave just enough to keep it going. The two men talked about their own generosity, but when the time came to act they found it hard to muster the same energy for Willie's work as for their own. Finally, it is incomplete to speak of the exchanges as though they are only material. It isn't only that outsiders want to be part of Willie's scene; Willie himself values the friendship and company of some people enough to forgive them for occasionally sloppy dealings. Some friendships are more important than others, and the tolerance extended is adjusted accordingly.

Restoring a Three-Banger

Nearly all the deals at Willie's are based on word of mouth and informal agreement. This system works for Willie as well as for his customers because he is able, for example, to estimate a job loosely and figure in the costs of his labor and the parts by his own private logic. The agreements between Willie and his customers are based on shared understandings of the "worth" of time and trust. Nearly all deals are made in good faith and are fulfilled to the satisfaction of both parties. But it is easy to idealize these kinds of face-to-face, often partly barter arrangements. After participating in a number of these relationships with neighboring traditional farmers, recent homesteaders, and people like Willie, I have come to a different understanding of Adam Smith's dictum that it is not through the love of humanity but through desire for self-betterment that the baker bakes his bread and so forth. Certainly after experiencing how a number of barter relationships evolved to either cash arrangements or carefully accounted hour-by-hour labor exchanges, my respect for an operation like Willie's, so dependent on informal expectations, has increased. There are times, however, when the system breaks down. The sheriff can be sent to collect a bad check, but there is no way to combat simple nonpayment except to exclude the offender from future dealings. Yet this is a severe penalty indeed. The following incident illustrates:

The old three-cylinder Saab station wagon had been sitting for years in a row of wrecked and abandoned Saabs in the back field. It was a 1961 or 1962, wrecked in the first years of its life, restored, driven for a decade, then retired to

Willie's. The cars sat carefully lined up, hidden by high weeds in the summer. Grass grew through the rusted floors and engine compartments, and because there is virtually no plastic in these cars they appeared to be slowly settling into union with the earth from which their materials had come. The old wagon caught my eye one of the first times Willie and I walked through the field. It looked vaguely like a spaceship from a Flash Gordon movie—tall, narrow, and sculptured, with funny little fins and round lines on the body. The car appeared to be salvageable, though the floorboards were rusted, one fender was wrinkled and bent beyond repair, the engine seized up, and the brake lines had been pirated for another car. I asked Willie if it could be put back on the road, but I don't think he even answered—of course it could! Just restorations, he said (they sounded so reasonable I thought for a while of restoring the car myself)—reversing the process of deterioration with renewal.

For years the wagon sat undisturbed. Finally, early in the spring one of the young women who had been coming to the shop with her old Saab throughout her college years decided to buy the wagon and help Willie restore it. I was at the shop the day it was brought in from the field, and I wondered. How many years had it been sinking more securely into the sod? How permanent was this arrangement between nature and machine?

Willie inched the old Jeep, which looked nearly as decrepit as the wagon, into place in front of the wreck. Its small winch was attached through the floor of the front end and then, straining with all its power, the Jeep pulled the car up out of the ground and moved gingerly ahead. Fleshy insects scurried about, frantic in the destruction of their world. The wagon rolled behind the Jeep, thump, thumping on tires that were irrevocably misshapen, and I sat on the musty seat looking through years of spiderwebs as I tried to steer. It was madness. The car belonged where it had been, and we had no right to disturb it.

Willie sold the car for $150 with the understanding that he would do the repairs for the price of parts and his time. The car would be worth a great deal of money if it was restored with the compulsiveness it deserved. I wondered, however, how far the job would go. The young woman cleaned the car out, began to replace the seats, discovered more problems than she had anticipated, and gave up. A month later she graduated from the local engineering college and moved to Connecticut, where it is rumored she bought a new Saab Turbo. In the meantime the car was sold to a man named Dick James who, Willie said, was raising his family on welfare.

I had never seen James in the shop before. Willie had known him for years, and there was a kind of abusive joviality that surrounds many of Willie's dealings with old acquaintances. James was a tall man with a protruding stomach, long sideburns, and a swarthy complexion, wearing a dirty ski hat in the middle of summer. He lived where he grew up, Willie said, in a trailer with a homemade house attached in the swampy and poor scrubland a few miles to the east.

James moved the job to the center of the shop, dominating the space and Willie's attention for a number of days when there was a lot of other work waiting to be done. But work on the wagon progressed quickly. They took the engine apart, replaced the broken parts, and put it back together and back into the car. They even sprayed it with orange engine paint. And an odd engine it was—a small fan inside a wire cage sat behind the engine blowing on a rear-mounted radiator. Willie replaced the wrinkled fender with one the same age miraculously intact in another corner of Willie's Saab heaven. He cut out the rotten metal in the floor and replaced it with steel plate he welded into place. The car had been wrecked at two thousand miles (twenty years before!) and had been driven with poorly aligned front window posts. Willie took out the Porta-Power and made them true. They adapted seats from a newer model by welding brackets to fit the new seats onto the floor. That Saturday they worked and worked to get the engine running, eventually installing a new ignition and rebuilding the carburetor. James asked Willie if he'd had his head on straight when he set the timing; there was a spark to the plugs and gas to the cylinders, but the engine only turned over and sounded interested.

I returned in the evening to find the same cast of characters. James had installed an eight-track stereo, violating the lovely interior by drilling holes that would permanently mar the dashboard. I'm sure he would have stuck a Chevy V-8 into the engine compartment if he'd been able. Willie told me he'd finally tried a different condenser, which had solved the engine problem; by hindsight he realized the new plugs were hotter than the originals, and with the cooler plugs the engine had fired. They started it up for me, and Willie bent over the engine revving the odd popcorn-popper-sounding engine; five minutes, eight minutes, garage filling with blue smoke from the oil and gas mixture the two-cycle engine burned; fine tuning the carbs, bleeding the heater, cleaning corroded fuse connections to bring various gauges and lights to life.

Willie had spent considerable time on the project, and the car had definitely increased in value. In part, Willie became involved because he derived satisfaction from seeing the old car back on the road. But it would be misleading to leave it at that; James was to sell his old LTD to pay for the Saab, then work off what he owed for Willie's labor and parts by disassembling some engines to salvage their good parts and cutting up some cars with his blowtorch so they could be taken to the junkyard. Willie expected a week's work from James, but I never saw him in the shop after that. I did see the car a few weeks later being driven through Potsdam by another man. James had sold it for $300 because it wasn't "fast enough," and he had not paid Willie any of the money he owed for the car or the repairs. It seemed like just another bad deal until I realized that in the long run James will pay. He's out of the circle. The next time he wants or needs something from Willie (a situation his poverty will force him into) Willie will *not* be there to make a deal unless the earlier debt has been paid.

These accounts tell about some of the more subtle aspects of social life in the shop. On one level there is a very simple system: customers come with their problems, and Willie agrees or does not agree to fix their machines. Prices are set and paid. If customers do not like the way Willie works or doubt his honesty, they do not come back. More important, they talk about their experience, influencing Willie's reputation in the community. Some people may be dissatisfied with the time some jobs take, for example, and an occasional customer complains about the price of a job. That there are more things to attend to in any given day than Willie is able to do, however, suggests that the community has, by and large, accepted his way of operating. That there is more work than Willie can possibly finish allows him to exercise his discretion in choosing what jobs he *will* take on. The conditions under which he chooses his work have to do, in part, with fulfillment of a subtle social reciprocity that is part of Willie's shop, but also part of the traditional way of life in the community.

This reciprocity has several elements. The most obvious is simply doing what you say you will do. Simple as this seems, several elements come into play. People may forget what they have said or remember different versions of the same account. Individuals may have a lot of initial enthusiasm for a deal, leading to an overgenerous promise that they are eventually unwilling to fulfill. Or a person may run into some hard luck and simply be unable to uphold his or her end of a deal. You can run short a time or two, but if you continually run short you will come to be known for that. Your work will still be done, but the prices will be higher, and you will have to wait. What might be more painful is that you will be spoken about that way by the community—held accountable through your reputation.

At a more subtle level, social reciprocity means being willing to help out when Willie needs a hand (although this is, surprisingly, minimal), or it might mean just stopping by a time or two to visit when you have no work to be done. It might mean being attentive rather than impatient when stories are told in the pauses between jobs. It surely means that you appreciate the quality of Willie's work and that you do not demean him by haggling over prices (which are always low). If you do these things over the years, you will have the opportunity to buy cheaply, or be given, a person's quite varied talents. You might also, incidentally, have the opportunity to establish a friendship. If you take advantage at a moment when you have the upper hand, or if you break one of the rules (unwritten, of course) that guide how things are done between neighbors, you may take yourself out of the circle of the shop for good. Finally, action is ongoing, and reputations, even when they achieve a certain inertia, are always in the process of being remade. Many are those who have erred in Willie's eyes, yet are slowly brought back into the group Willie works and lives with.

Epilogue

I returned from Willie's shop on a Saturday afternoon in late January. It had been cold, and machines had been breaking. I'm not even sure the weather had had any effect on the wheel bearing in my car, but for whatever mystery of its own, within five minutes a chirping in the left rear wheel led to a couple of resounding SNAPS! and the bearing disintegrated, ruining the wheel hub in the process. The parts had to come from Connecticut, and they were expensive. When the parts arrived Willie fixed the car (reshaping the axle with a file and thus saving me the $400 for a new one); then on a test drive he noticed a clunking on the front passenger side and replaced a shock rubber to correct that.

He'd just finished fixing the heater motor that had burned out in his own car. There were none on the junkers that surround the shop, but he'd discovered that the windshield wiper motor from a different model of Saab, seven years older, had the same bushing size though a different shaft length and diameter. He'd taken the two motors apart, made a new shaft on the lathe, and built one good motor from the parts. He was sitting in the car when I arrived, smiling as his hand felt the heat rising from the defroster vents.

Nothing changes at the shop. Each job is different; all are performed with the same care. There is a reassuring feeling to the repetition; it seems as natural (and sometimes hard) as the seasons themselves. Willie knows, indeed, that each season brings its own work.

I linger for some hours. Although the sense of repetition is strong, there is talk of change. I sense Willie's universe shrinking. Ralph, with whom he had made himself healthy through work, died a couple of seasons ago; Brad, for whom he had been a master (if incorrigible) Saab mechanic, went a season before that. We talk about spring, for the winter seems to have broken by late January, and Willie tells me yet another farm in the neighborhood has gone out of business. "Soon," he says, "there won't *be* spring work." The claim is not as exaggerated as it sounds. Agriculture is disappearing from the region; houses are empty, machines sit rusting and disused, like dejected sentinels guarding a forgotten landscape. Several of Willie's own friends have fallen on hard times. We almost lost Raymond the summer before. He'd been in the hospital for a month, and when he stabilized his diabetes had taken his eyesight to the point that he must be driven and led. "He only sees shadows," Willie says; "only shadows." Bill, another friend, has Alzheimer's disease and is deteriorating fast. I say that he seems childlike, or like a teenager with irrational enthusiasms. "The other day," Willie answers, "he drove over here; I don't know how he found it. He got ready to leave and he says, 'Now, do I go right or left to get home?'" Willie tells me he called Bill's wife, who came and led him home.

I give Willie news from the publisher on the progress of my manuscript. The readers' reports have been positive; the project appears to be nearing completion. Willie is interested but a little distant. It does not seem to concern him much. Unlike someone in the public eye, who makes sure his authorized biography contains the image he wants projected for the future, Willie knows that through his work his reputation will continue to live in the neighborhood. Beyond that—well, there should be a record, Willie says, of this kind of work. It will be gone soon enough.

Willie's comment brings to the surface the most basic question of my book, the relation of the individual to society. Willie's world shrinks as even the North Country slowly modernizes. More and more people forgo the pleasures of a well-engineered but persnickety Saab for a boring but reliable Japanese car. The concept of use without ownership—the lease—gains currency even here. Virtually all automobiles are becoming so complicated that sometimes without specialized training and exotic equipment even Willie's hand, ear, and eye cannot fathom their workings. The farms that remain tend to trade in their equipment to get maximum depreciation allowances and investment credits. And what is Willie's place in this new age?

I think of Lothar-Gunther Buchheim's (1975) description of German submarine duty during World War II. Buchheim, a journalist, tells of sitting in a submarine stranded on the ocean floor in eight hundred feet of water—essential parts broken after a long and terrible battle, the mechanical systems of the ship seemingly beyond repair. Thus they sit, awaiting death as they foul the air with their own breath. The only way out is to make parts to salvage the huge battery that runs the ship underwater, to clear the hull of the water that holds them on the bottom, to fix the motors and compressors. The chief engineer strips wiring from one end of the ship to repair the other; shafts are bent back into shape with hammers and levers. Parts are made from scratch. If you were lucky, it would be Willie working there in the hold.

But there are fewer and fewer broken submarines lying on the bottom of the ocean waiting for the bricoleur's hand. Or at least that appears to be the case. Places like the North Country change more slowly than the indicators suggest. The weather, the poverty, and the isolation will see to Willie's continued role. But we should also consider Willie's method in the context of the technological complexity that now seems to be everywhere. The layman's sense that no one mind can comprehend the conceptual shape of particular technologies is confirmed by accounts such as Perrow's description of the *normal* accident at Three Mile Island (1984), Kidder's description of designing a computer (1981), or events such

as the explosion of the space shuttle or the debate over Star Wars technology. Willie's method tells us we have come from a technology that can be confronted by a single human mind. As we have moved beyond this stage we face an imbalance in the human/machine relationship that makes us impotent captives of our own creations. I look at Willie's world to see one universe in wonderful detail; but I also look to call attention to the larger change that surrounds us all.

Notes

1. The population in New York's sixty-two counties ranges from 3 people per square mile in Hamilton County, in the heart of the Adirondacks, to 62,086 people per square mile in New York County of New York City. This vast range makes a statewide average meaningless; for rough comparison, most rural counties in New York State have between 200 and 800 people per square mile. Saint Lawrence County, with 41 people per square mile, has considerably fewer than nearly any other non-Adirondack county. Part of the reason for its low population density is that the southern part of the county includes the foothills of the Adirondack Mountains, but the nonmountainous rural areas are also sparsely populated. The population growth rate between 1970 and 1980 was 2 percent; while a few counties in the state lost population, most grew by considerably more than Saint Lawrence (U.S. Bureau of the Census 1982; Webster's *New Geographical Dictionary*, 1980 edition). These facts, particularly the size of the county, (nearly twice the size of the next largest in the state), its population density, its geographical isolation from other regions, and the weather, give the area a genuine regional identity.

2. North Country agriculture is largely fluid milk production, which began about 1900. For about forty years following the Civil War the principal market product was cheese. The original cash crops (from about 1815, the approximate time of white settlement) were whiskey and ash, followed in the mid-nineteenth century by sheep. Sheep have staged a partial comeback in current North Country agriculture (Saint Lawrence County Cooperative Extension Association 1981, 6). Saint Lawrence County contains 1,770,880 acres of land, of which 629,000 (35.5%) are forest preserve. At one time nearly all of the remaining 1,141,880 acres was in agricultural production. At present the area being farmed has declined to less than 500,000 acres, about 40 percent of the acreage used earlier (ibid., 11). In 1925 there were 7,583 farms in Saint Lawrence County, most of them between 50 and 260 acres, with an average farm size of 133.5 acres (U.S. Bureau of the Census 1927). By 1978, the most recent year for which data are available, there were 1,834 farms, about 75 percent fewer than in 1925, and the average size had risen only to 273 acres, about twice the 1925 average (ibid., 12, 16).

3. Glaser and Straus (1967) suggest that the researcher should formulate hypotheses tentatively and continually reform through ongoing observation. In this way theory is *grounded* in the data. Glaser and Straus's ideas have given ethnographers stimulation and insight for nearly twenty years, and I think they will continue to do so for the next few decades at least.

4. Peter Berger and his colleagues (1973) have described the extension of the consciousness of modernization into almost all pockets of Western and non-Western culture. Still, some areas are "left behind," suggesting they support no less than a different form of consciousness. In a modest way this is my argument in relation to the North Country.

5. This is in contrast to the ethnoscience method, which influenced me greatly earlier in my career. The ethnoscience method is summarized in a number of places, but very well in *The Ethnographic Interview* (1979) by my late and deeply missed teacher James Spradley. Ethnoscience leads to taxonomies of language, which are considered to reflect the pattern of shared meanings. Although I find ethnoscience useful because it places the researcher in the position of student vis-à-vis the informant, I have not used it as a method in this study because of the limitations of analyzing one individual's language as representative of the language of a cultural group and because in this setting the vocabulary is not different enough to warrant taxonomic analysis. In this case it has been more fruitful to concentrate on learning the *meanings* of the words Willie uses—words that are, by themselves, not an elaborate vocabulary. My goal, however, is squarely in the tradition of ethnography: to gain the point of view, the reality-as-experienced, of my subject.

6. Becker writes: "Qualitative data and analytic procedures, in contrast to quantitative ones, are difficult to present adequately. Statistical data can be summarized in tables, and descriptive measures of various kinds and the methods by which they are handled can often be accurately reported in the space required to print a formula. The data of participant observation do not lend themselves to such a ready summary. They frequently consist of many different kinds of observations which cannot be simply categorized and counted without losing some of their value as evidence. . . . a possible solution to this problem . . . is a description of the natural history of our conclusions, presenting the evidence as it came to the attention of the observer during the successive stages of his conceptualization of the problem. The term 'natural history' implies not the presentation of every datum, but only the characteristic forms data took at each stage of the research." (1958, 659).

7. These include Margaret Mead and Gregory Bateson's *Balinese Character* (1942), a juxtaposition of photographs and cultural analysis that many feel has never been equaled. John Collier and Anibal Buitron collaborated on *The Awakening Valley* (1949), a visual ethnography of Ecuadorian village life. Robert Gardner and Karl Heider's *Gardens of War* (1969) parallels the

film *Dead Birds* and Heider's more typical ethnographic treatment of the Dani of New Guinea. John Berger and Jean Mohr have collaborated on three projects: *A Seventh Man* (1975), about migrant labor in Europe; *A Fortunate Man* (1967), which describes the life and work of a country doctor in England; and *Another Way of Telling* (1982), which contains several short explorations of how photographs and texts may be combined and a long series of photographs that constitute a fictional biography of a European peasant woman. Frank Cancian's *Another Place* (1974) is a visual ethnography of Mexican peasant life. Deborah Barndt's *Education and Social Change: A Photographic Study of Peru* (1980) shows how photographs have been used in literacy programs. Michael Smith's *Spirit World* (1983) portrays the rituals and festivals of black New Orleans culture, and Bruce Jackson's *Killing Time* (1977) presents life in an Arkansas penitentiary. Robert Coles and Alex Harris have collaborated on two studies, *The Last and the First Eskimos* (1977) and *The Old Ones of New Mexico* (1973), about elderly people in rural New Mexico. My own study of railroad tramps, *Good Company* (1982), includes photographs as a parallel statement to the text. Several of these book-length studies, as well as several shorter works, are excerpted in Howard S. Becker's *Exploring Society Photographically* (1981) and Jon Wagner's *Images of Information* (1979).

8. I am thinking of such works as W. Eugene Smith and Aileen Smith's *Minamata* (1975), a visual and narrative account of mercury pollution and the social movement that rose to stop it in rural Japan; Danny Lyon's *Conversations with the Dead* (1969), which presents life inside a Texas prison; Roswitha Hecke's *Lovelife: Scenes with Irene* (1982), the day and night life of a European prostitute; Ethan Hoffman and John McCoy's *Concrete Mama* (1981), on the effects of liberal reform in a Washington prison; Michael Mathers's *Sheepherders: Men Alone* (1975) and *Riding the Rails* (1973), each about a different aspect of migrant life in the West; Bill Owens's *Suburbia* (1973) and *Our Kind of People* (1975) and Mary Lloyd Estrin's *To the Manor Born* (1979), which taken together present daily life of suburbanites and the upper class in America; and Marc Riboud's *Visions of China* (1981), which shows in comparative photographs the remarkable social change going on inside China.

Bill Ganzel rephotographed several Farm Security Administration photographers' work (the work of Dorothea Lange, Russell Lee, and other FSA photographers is also useful work done by documentarians) in *Dust Bowl Descent* (1984), telling a great deal about the changes brought over thirty years in specific parts of America. *Tulsa* (1971) and *Teenage Lust* (1983) by Larry Clark show a group of his friends who are amphetamine addicts and portray teenage crime and sex. Jacob Holdt's *American Pictures* (1985), which includes seven hundred photographs the Danish author took during a five-year subsistence-level hitchhiking trip through the United States, is the most penetrating portrait of the American underclass that has ever been done. Finally, Bernard Stehle's *Incurably Romantic* (1985) presents in photographs and interviews the romantic and sexual lives of those living in an institution for the chronically disabled. The relationship among these books, which I have selected from the large number of photographic books done on "sociological topics" and "visual sociology," deserves a separate treatment, for it is a complex web of purposes, methods, and publishing intentions. I have chosen these examples because, though not done by social scientists, they represent the kind of working relationship that fieldworkers try to establish with their subjects. This empathy between subject and photographer, the same empathy sought by the fieldworker, is found in the photographs themselves and in the sometimes minimal text that accompanies them. But while the empathy may be the same, the theory that guides it may not represent sociological understanding. This can be a difficult omission to accept.

9. Other studies using photo elicitation have been done primarily in cross-cultural research. Sprague (1978) used both his own and culture members' photographs in a brief but fascinating examination of how the Yoruba of western Nigeria see themselves and their values. Ximena Bunster B. (1978) applied the photo elicitation method to her study of how proletarian mothers in Peru perceived, structured, and evaluated their worlds. Barndt (1980), in one of the only book-length studies that relies heavily on the photo elicitation technique, used photos not only to study a community of rural migrants in Lima, Peru, but also to implement through literacy campaigns the radical pedagogy of Paulo Freire. Victor Caldarola (1985) described a detailed photographic research program, which includes the photo elicitation interview, in his review of how he and his wife studied duck-egg farming in an Indonesian village. Curry (1986) uses the photo elicitation method in a study of college wrestlers to understand how athletes see their sports role. William Foote Whyte (1984, 105–8) briefly discusses how he has used photographs in several research projects to discover how his subjects defined aspects of their work lives. In 1925 Margaret Mead is reported to have used still photographs made during the filming of Robert Flaherty's dramatized documentary *Monana* to elicit responses from Samoan children (De Brigard 1974, 31). Bob Saltzman used a type of photo elicitation in his photographs of inmates and workers at the New Mexico penitentiary. Saltzman returned his color prints, mounted on cardboard with wide margins around them, to the

subjects. They added whatever comments, drawings, or markings they felt the photographs needed to reflect their own interpretations of them. This project is summarized in Engel (1985).

Stephanie Krebs (1975) has detailed the methods of motion picture elicitation, another potentially rich technique that has been largely unused.

Photo elicitation is also related to reflexive documentary or ethnographic filmmaking. In reflexive films, those being filmed become in part the makers of the films. In Jean Rouch and Edward Morin's film *Chronicle of a Summer*, the subjects, after revealing their hopes, dreams, and general psychological condition, were filmed watching the film and commenting on its accuracy. The reflexive or participatory documentary is described by MacDougall (1974) and Nichols (1983); MacDougall's recent reflexive films are analyzed in MacBean (1983). Asch, Asch, and Connor's reflexive film on a Balinese spirit medium is thoroughly described in their text (forthcoming).

10. Generally decisions regarding a book's final form—the placing of the photographs in relation to the text—are the responsibility of the publisher's art director or designer. The decisions are based on a combination of aesthetic and practical considerations. As a result the books are generally "well designed"—meaning they communicate the essential information in an aesthetically pleasing manner. On the other hand, the precise positioning of text and image, or a particular reproduction quality wanted by the author/photographer, may not be achieved. One small and very powerful book in which the text/photo relationship has an almost movielike quality is Adelman and Hall's *On and off the Street* (1970), which presents small incidents in the relationship between a black boy and his white friend. Of the numerous photographic/textual essays that create a particularly harmonious interrelation of text and image, several stand out. Jan Saudek (1982) presents a series of photographic allegories and text that tell of the life of a man who leaves his home country. Milan Kundera's text and Josef Koudelka's photographs of the Russian invasion of Czechoslovakia (Koudelka and Kundera 1984) are organized in such a way that the composition becomes part of the message.

11. Howard Becker (1966) describes the rationale for the case study method in sociology and suggests several reasons why the case study, or life history, has fallen into general disuse in social research. The "Chicago school" is associated, in its early history, with case studies such as Nels Anderson's *The Hobo* (1923) and Clifford R. Shaw's *The Jack-Roller* (1930). Becker argues that though the case study does not produce typical social scientific "data," it provides important information because it ex-

plores the point of view of the subject. It is easier, Becker suggests, to understand background information—the community or institutional context—as an actual social process when the events of a single social actor are seen in detail.

The case study has had a diminished role in sociology, in Becker's view, for several reasons. The "subjectivity" of the information (meaning that it derives from a single subject's in-depth reports) detracts, for many sociologists, from its usefulness. But perhaps more important that the actual character of the data are more structural reasons that surround their production. The case study does not produce the kind of information that is easily defended in a doctoral dissertation or published in professional journals, or that is likely to generate research funding. Case studies take a long time and require researchers to work in eclectic rather than explicit fashion. Finally, Becker reminds us that the attention of the discipline has turned away from local ethnography or community studies at least partly because professional sociologists usually live in cities and frequently move from job to job. Such a life-style does not produce the kind of local knowledge that typically leads to the case study. Although Becker's comments are now twenty years old, I find them relevant in explaining the contours of contemporary sociological research. Recent trends that have led to something of a rebirth of the case study include the evolution of several graduate departments of sociology that are sympathetic to sociological ethnography, the publication of several sociological journals committed to methods that include the case study, and the continued interest of leading university presses in the case study or, more broadly, sociological ethnography. At the same time, anthropologists and folklorists are now often working in areas that were previously considered the privileged terrain of the sociologist. Michael Owen Jones's *The Hand Made Object and Its Maker* (1975), for example, while formally a study of "folklife," can also be read as a penetrating analysis of the phenomenological character of work in its community context.

PART ONE: THE NATURE OF WORK

1. Smith (1981, 98).

2. See Smith (1981, 113) and Smith in Knauth (1974, 7).

3. Lynn White, Jr., shows that other important technological changes characterized the ninth century, including the development of the nailed horseshoe, efficient horse harnesses, and the continuing development of the heavy plow. These technological breakthroughs increased agriculture productivity and brought a

corresponding increase in population and, White suggests, the beginning of the Western attitude of human domination over nature. The development of the nailed horseshoe and the consequent evolution of horse-based agricultural technology expanded the role of the ironworker to that of farrier and maker and fixer of agricultural machinery (1962, 56–57).

4. While it is not clear whether the settlers put up with the smith because of his contribution to the community or because they were afraid of him, it *is* clear that his skills were indispensable and that he was one of the least desirable characters in the community. Part of this fear of the smith came from the belief that he used black magic (Berry 1977, 49–51).

5. The elderly men and women Glassie interviewed in his study of a village in Northern Ireland also believed that iron and steel possessed magical powers—for example, that "a ghost won't go near steel, a turf spade, like a prayer, will protect you, and the people in the past stuck steel in their clothes when traveling dark, haunted routes. Steel tongs were placed across the cradles of infants to prevent them from being stolen by fairies. . . . an iron hoop was used in the attempt to retrieve a man from fairy land" (1982, 579). A seventeenth-century Irish canto includes the lines:

> Directly under Bridget's cross
> Was firmly nail'd the shoe of horse
> On threshold, that the house might be
> From witches, thieves, and devils free.
> (Glassie 1982, 378)

Glassie cites Lloyd Laing, *Celtic Britain* (New York: Scribner's, 1979), pp. 44–48, and Alwyn Rees and Brinley Rees, *Celtic Heritage* (Levittown, N.Y.: Transatlantic, 1975), pp. 252–53, on the ancient power of the smith. See Glassie's footnote 2 to chap. 22 (1982, 783).

6. Pascal Boyer shows (1983) that blacksmiths in African societies are either despised or honored; they are never thought of as ordinary craftsmen; Anne De Sales (1981) studies how the blacksmith/shaman relationship among the Yakut of Siberia contradicts the elder/junior status of these roles. David F. Lancy (1980) shows how one of the roles of the smith, that of medicine man, is learned in a slash-and-burn society in West Africa, and Dona Richards (1981) explains in penetrating detail the significance of the spiritual side of the blacksmith's work in African societies.

7. There are few studies of the smith in North America. An exception is Jean-Claude Dupont's (1979) study of the background, training, and economic and social position of the French Canadian blacksmith from the seventeenth century to the present. Dupont also provides a general history of blacksmithing, as well as discussing the folklore that has surrounded the smith in French Canada and Europe. Jeanette Lasansky (1980) has presented a brief but well-illustrated account of the evolution of the blacksmith from the mid-eighteenth century to the 1930s in rural Pennsylvania.

8. The literature on the alienation of the worker in industrial society is vast. Hall (1986, 103–10) has written a comprehensive survey of how sociologists have operationalized and measured the concept in research in various modern work settings. Such an abstract concept, however, has not easily found its way into variable analysis. For example, alienation has been thought of by some as something as broad as "the lack of job satisfaction," while others have followed Blauner's (1964) lead in breaking the concept into dimensions of powerlessness, meaninglessness, isolation, and self-estrangement. But many have quarreled with how these terms have been conceptualized and measured.

The modern analysis of "alienation" derives from Marx, including the following often-quoted passage in the *Manuscripts of 1844* (in Tucker 1972, 72–78): "The worker is related to the *product of his labour* as to an *alien* object. For on this premise it is clear that the more the worker spends on himself, the more powerful the alien objective world becomes which he creates over-against himself, the poorer he himself—his inner world—becomes, the less belongs to him as his own. . . . The *alienation* of the worker in his product means not only that his labour becomes an object, an *external* existence, but that it exists *outside him*, independently, as something alien to him, and that it becomes a power of its own confronting him; it means that the life which he has conferred on the object confronts him as something hostile and alien . . . the estrangement is manifested not only in the result but in the *act of production—within the producing activity* itself. . . .

". . . labour is *external* to the worker, i.e., it does not belong to his essential being; that in his work, therefore, he does not affirm himself but denies himself, does not feel content but unhappy, does not develop freely his physical and mental energy but mortifies his body and ruins his mind. The worker therefore only feels himself outside his work, and in his work feels outside his work. . . . the external character of labour for the worker appears in the fact that it is not his own, but someone else's, that it does not belong to him, that in it he belongs, not to himself, but to another.

"It is just in the working-up of the objective world, therefore, that man first really proves himself to be a *species being*. This production is his active species life. Through and because of this production, nature appears as *his* work and his reality. The object of labour is, therefore, the *objectification of man's species life*: for he duplicates himself not only, as in consciousness, intellectually, but also actively, in reality, and therefore he contemplates himself in a world that he has created. In tearing away from man the object of his production, therefore, estranged labour tears from him his *species* life, his real species objectivity, and transforms his advantage over animals into the disadvantage that his inorganic body, nature, is taken from him.

". . . An immediate consequence of the fact that man is estranged from the product of his labour, from his life-activity, from his species being is the *estrangement of man from man*."

Marx, of course, was describing the experience of the then new industrial proletariat. Passages such as these, however, have come to stand metaphorically for much of the experience of work in modern society, whether in a factory or a bureaucracy. Willie's working life has been spent in one of the niches where skilled labor and control of one's work are still possible. His attitude toward the issue was revealed in several conversations about his friends who do industrial work in the neighboring town. Although their wages are high, the intrinsic satisfaction these workers derive from their jobs is at best minimal. Several of these people regularly do their own projects in Willie's shop, and Willie sees their interest as a need to find an outlet for the mechanical inventiveness that is missing from their working lives.

9. Gerth and Mills suggest that for Weber "the extent and direction of 'rationalization' is . . . measured negatively in terms of the degree to which magical elements of thought are displaced, or positively by the extent to which ideas gain in systematic coherence and naturalistic consistency" (1946, 51). Weber's use of "rationalization" is associated primarily with the study of the evolution of bureaucracy and countervailing forces of charisma. The concept, however, has been used by sociologists since Weber to mean several things. For those of us who hope to work toward a clearer definition of concepts, this is a dismaying circumstance. But Levine (1985, 142–98) shows us in penetrating detail that even Weber did not distinguish clearly between types of rationalization. The lack of definition, Levine tells us, "can be seen expressing his considered ambivalence toward any effort to create systematic conceptual inventories. While Weber consid-

ered it worthwhile to secure univocal meanings in particular expository contexts, he also believed that the meaning of terms might legitimately shift from one context to another" (p. 152). My own use of the concept, inspired by Weber, develops in a very small example an analysis consistent, I believe, with the general direction of Weber's thought.

10. The deskilling of manual work in the industrial period was identified by Marx throughout his analysis of the development of capitalism and developed as a separate argument by Braverman (1974; see particularly chs. 4 and 20). The concept of "deskilling" has also been applied to several other aspects of modern work, notably to clerical work (Davies 1982; Glenn and Feldberg 1977) and even managerial work, as Lasch (1979) speaks about the loss of the craft of management and its replacement by the "seductive" manager.

11. Ivan Illich (1977) suggests that the evolution of professionalization toward an ever-increasing mandate in private life is "disabling." While this argument is usually made in reference to health and education, I think it can also be applied to servicing the made environment we live in.

12. See Weizenbaum (1976), particularly his final chapter, "The Imperialism of Instrumental Reasoning."

13. David Sudnow, an ethnomethodologist, in *The Ways of the Hand* (1978), fashions a language to describe the knowledge in the hands occurring to a jazz pianist. In *Talk's Body* (1979) he experiments with a typewriter keyboard, fashioning a more abstract "language" to describe the "work" of the hands. Carla Needleman, in *The Work of Craft* (1979), describes in a more conventional manner the nature of her hand knowledge as a potter.

14. Zerubavel writes that "the temporal rigidity of modern work schedules is one of the key structural characteristics of modern social organization" (1981, xv). Applebaum (1984) identifies this temporal rigidity as a defining characteristic of modern work and describes the difficulties of cultures caught between a traditional time sense—in which time is embedded in tasks—and a modern time accounting.

15. The original formulation is found in Taylor (1911) and forms the basis of Braverman's (1974) analysis.

16. Zerubavel develops the idea of durational time aspects throughout his published work. See especially *Hidden Rhythms: Schedules and Calendars in Social Life* (1981).

17. See Zerubavel (1981, 11), particularly his citation (note 30) of Georg Simmel's *Philosophy of Money* (pp. 485–91).

18. Zerubavel quotes Lynch: "As men free themselves from

submission to the external cycles of nature, relying more often on self-created and variable social cycles, they increasingly risk internal disruption" (1981, 12).

PART TWO: CONTEXTS OF WORK

1. Marx's *The German Ideology* (1970) is a strong statement arguing for the role of social class in determining consciousness.

2. See chaps. 1 and 6 of Berger's 1981 study.

3. Wendell Berry's 1977 book is an eloquent and powerfully reasoned defense of the small farm based on modest scales of technology. Schumacher's (1973) study of "appropriate technology" has been a model for agricultural experiments with small, adaptable technology both here and in the Third World.

4. See Stadtfeld (1972, 152–74) for an overview of the evolution of agricultural technology in a rural neighborhood in Michigan. A similar evolution existed in New York's North Country.

5. A detailed study of the effects of contour plowing and related farming practices on a farm neighborhood is found in Herbert Harper's 1954 thesis, "Soil Conservation Problems in a Transitional Area."

6. The idea that parental authority is traditionally rooted in family work systems, and that it has been largely displaced by industrial capitalism—that is, the creation of wage labor and the subsequent removal of the father from productive activity in the house—is a central theme in modern sociology. In *Middletown* (1924), Robert and Helen Lynd described the effect of these industrial processes one generation after they had taken place.

7. As Bruce Jackson (1985) points out, the process of categorization that separates folklore from nonfolklore is largely arbitrary. Richard Dorson adds: "Folklorists are beginning to accept 'true' stories, personal narratives, and conversational dialogues as grist for *their* mill, on the premise that all kinds of impromptu story telling deserve attention. The orally told tale is, after all, a prime concern of folklore scholars, so why should they decide apriori what kinds of tales the folk should tell for their consideration?" Dorson does suggest, however, that to be considered folklore the stories should form a corpus (1981, 108).

8. This is properly part of the tradition of occupational folklore. See Messenger's 1975 study of the folklore of linen mills in Northern Ireland in the early decades of the twentieth century (though she calls her study "industrial folklore" to distinguish it from "occupational folklore"). See also Archie Green, *Only a Miner* (1972); Mody Boatright, *Folklore of the Oil Industry* (1963); Mody Boatright and William Owens, *Tales from the Derrick Floor* (1982); George Korson's *Minstrels of the Mine Patch* (1938), *Coal Dust on the Fiddle* (1943), and *Black Rock* (1960), which Messenger cites in her study. Richard Bauman's 1972 paper studied the folklore of Canadian fishermen as it had traditionally been delivered on winter evenings in general stores on isolated islands off the southwest coast of Nova Scotia. Ferris (1982) studies the folklore of craftworkers who make such things as baskets, musical instruments, quilts, and needlework.

Dorson's study of people's spoken interpretations of their life in the industrial northwestern corner of Indiana (1981) is particularly interesting in relation to Willie's storytelling. Much of Dorson's study is concerned with the "folklore of steel"—workers' idealization of the "old days," grisly recounting of industrial accidents, workers' theft as a form of protest about their working conditions, and the cataloging of odd or colorful characters in the workplace. On the whole, however, Dorson does not analyze the themes of the stories beyond suggesting that they reflect, in general, the "hatefulness of industrial work" (1981, 108).

9. See David Halle (1984, 145–47) for an exploration of the attitudes of contemporary blue-collar factory workers toward their work. LeMasters (1974, 19–35) shows how those in the skilled construction trades, who are actually craftsmen handling heavy equipment, find satisfaction and fulfillment in their work situations.

10. In slightly more detail: an individual, guided by an uncomplicated view of right and wrong, is confronted by moral choices that themselves are often complex. Typical representatives of law and order may not be acting on the side of "the good" or "the just." The individual must sort out his confusion and must act. The actions may seem on the surface to contradict taken-for-granted notions of "the good"—the means may be violent; they may temporarily suspend lawfulness. In general, however, "the law" is "good," but particular laws, particular policemen, particular judges, and often bureaucracies are not. One must persevere because in the end the higher good is always achieved. The final confrontation is between the individual and the representative of the higher good. In the confrontation the individual alone presents logic and evidence to vindicate himself for the original infraction and the events that may have happened in the meantime as he "takes law into his own hands." Kenny Rogers's song "Coward of the County" is a good example. The narrator won't fight because of a promise to his father, who died in jail. Finally, when his wife is gang raped by a bunch of hoodlums he whips them in hand-to-hand combat and then returns to tell his father's picture, "Sometimes you've got to fight to be a man." Similar themes are common in popular cinema.

References

Adelman, Bob, and Susan Hall. 1970. *On and off the street.* New York: Viking.

Anderson, Nels. 1923. *The hobo.* Chicago: University of Chicago Press.

Applebaum, Herbert, ed. 1984. *Work in non-market and transitional societies.* Albany: State University of New York Press.

Asch, Timothy, Patsy Asch, and Linda Connor. N.d. *Jero Tapakan, a Balinese healer: an ethnographic film monograph.* Cambridge: Cambridge University Press, forthcoming.

Barndt, Deborah. 1980. *Education and social change: A photographic study of Peru.* Dubuque, Iowa: Kendall Hunt.

Baskin, John. 1976. *New Burlington: The life and death of an American village.* New York: W. W. Norton.

Bauman, Richard. 1972. The La Have Island general store: Sociability and verbal art in a Nova Scotia community. Paper presented at the Conference on the Ethnography of Speaking, University of Texas.

Becker, Howard S. 1958. Problems of inference and proof. *American Sociological Review* 23 (December): 652–60.

———. 1964. Problems in the publication of field studies. In *Reflections on community studies,* ed. A. Vidich, J. Bensman, and M. Stein. New York: John Wiley.

———. 1966. Introduction. In *The jack-roller: A delinquent boy's own story,* ed. Clifford R. Shaw. Chicago: University of Chicago Press.

———. 1974. Photography and sociology. *Studies in the Anthropology of Visual Communication* 1, no. 1: 3–26.

———, ed. 1981. *Exploring society photographically.* Chicago: University of Chicago Press.

Bell, Daniel. 1956. *Work and its discontents: The cult of efficiency in America.* Boston: Beacon Press.

Bensman, J., and R. Lilienfeld. 1973. *Craft and consciousness: Occupational technique and the development of world images.* New York: John Wiley.

Berger, Bennett, 1981. *The survival of a counterculture: Ideological work and everyday life among rural communards.* Berkeley: University of California Press.

Berger, John, and Jean Mohr. 1967. *The fortunate man: The story of a country doctor.* New York: Holt, Rinehart and Winston.

———. 1975. *A seventh man: Migrant workers in Europe.* New York: Viking.

———. 1982. *Another way of telling.* New York: Pantheon.

Berger, Peter L., et al. 1973. *Homeless mind: Modernization and consciousness.* New York: Random House.

Berry, Francis, ed. 1977. *I tell of Greenland: An edited translation of the Sauðarkrokur manuscripts.* Boston: Routledge and Kegan Paul.

Berry, Wendell. 1977. *The unsettling of America: Culture and agriculture.* San Francisco: Sierra Club.

Bittner, Egon. 1983. Technique and the conduct of life. *Social Problems* 30, no. 3: 249–61.

Blauner, Robert. 1964. *Alienation and freedom.* Chicago: University of Chicago Press.

Blythe, Ronald. 1969. *Akenfield.* New York: Random House.

Boatright, Mody. 1963. *Folklore of the oil industry.* Dallas: Southern Methodist University Press.

Boatright, Mody, and William Owens. 1982. *Tales from the derrick floor: A people's history of the oil industry.* Lincoln: University of Nebraska Press.

Boyer, Pascal. 1983. The status of blacksmiths and its symbolic justifications—a cognitive hypothesis. *Africa* 53, no. 1: 44–63.

Braudel, Fernand. 1981. *The structures of everyday life.* Vol. 1. New York: Harper and Row.

Braverman, Harry. 1974. *Labor and monopoly capital: The degradation of work in the twentieth century.* New York: Monthly Review Press.

Buchheim, Lothar-Gunther. 1975. *The Boat.* New York: Alfred A. Knopf.

Bunster B., Ximena. 1978. Talking pictures: A study of proletarian mothers in Lima, Peru. *Studies in the Anthropology of Visual Communication* 5, no. 1: 37–55.

Caldarola, Victor J. 1985. Visual contexts: A photographic research method in anthropology. *Studies in Visual Communication* 11 (Summer): 33–55.

Cancian, Frank. 1974. *Another place.* San Francisco: Scrimshaw Press.

Clark, Larry. 1971. *Tulsa.* New York: Lustrum Press.

———. 1983. *Teenage lust.* New York: privately published.

Coles, Robert. 1973. *The old ones of New Mexico.* Albuquerque: University of New Mexico Press.

Coles, Robert, and Alex Harris. 1977. *The last and the first Eskimos.* New York: New York Graphic Society.

Collier, John. 1967. *Visual anthropology: Photography as a research method.* New York: Holt, Rinehart and Winston.

Collier, John, and Anibal Buitron. 1949. *The awakening valley.* Chicago: University of Chicago Press.

Curry, Timothy Jon. 1984. Photographic comparisons as a visual technique for the social sciences. Paper presented at the Visual Sociology Association conference, Rochester, New York.

———. 1986. A visual method of studying sports: The photo-elicitation interview. *Sociology of Sport Journal* 3: 204–16.

Davies, Margery W. 1982. *Woman's place is at the typewriter: Office work and office workers, 1870–1930*. Philadelphia: Temple University Press.

De Brigard, Emile. 1974. The history of ethnographic film. In *Principles of visual anthropology*, ed. Paul Hockings. The Hague: Mouton.

De Sales, Anne. 1981. The blacksmith-shaman relationship among the Yakut of Siberia. *Homme* 21, no. 2: 35–61.

Dorson, Richard M. 1981. *Land of the millrats*. Cambridge: Harvard University Press.

Dupont, Jean-Claude. 1979. *L'artisan forgeron*. Quebec: Presses de l'Université Laval.

Engel, Nancy Timmes. 1985. Messages from prison. *Popular Photography*, pp. 66–69, 144.

Estrin, Mary Lloyd. 1979. *To the manor born*. New York: New York Graphic Society.

Evans, George Ewart. 1966. *The pattern under the plough*. London: Faber and Faber.

Ferris, William. 1982. *Local color: A sense of place in folk art*. New York: McGraw-Hill.

Ganzel, Bill. 1984. *Dust bowl descent*. Lincoln: University of Nebraska Press.

Gardner, Robert, and Karl Heider. 1969. *Gardens of war*. New York: Random House.

Gerth, Hans, and C. W. Mills, eds. 1946. *From Max Weber: Essays in sociology*. New York: Oxford University Press.

Glaser, Barney G., and Anselm L. Straus. 1967. *The discovery of grounded theory: Strategies for qualitative research*. Chicago: Aldine.

Glassie, Henry. 1982. *Passing the time in Ballymenone: Culture and history of an Ulster community*. Philadelphia: University of Pennsylvania Press.

Glenn, Evelyn, and Roslyn Feldberg. 1977. Degraded and deskilled: The proletarianization of clerical work. *Social Problems* 25 (October): 25–64.

Green, Archie. 1972. *Only a miner*. Urbana: University of Illinois Press.

Hall, Richard. 1986. *Dimensions of work*. Beverly Hills: Sage.

Halle, David. 1984. *America's working man*. Chicago: University of Chicago Press.

Harper, Douglas. 1982. *Good company*. Chicago: University of Chicago Press.

Harper, Herbert H. 1954. Soil conservation problems in a transitional area. M.A. thesis, Macalester College.

Hecke, Roswitha. 1982. *Lovelife: Scenes with Irene*. Munich: Rogner and Bernhard.

Hoffman, Ethan, and John McCoy. 1981. *Concrete mama*. Columbia: University of Missouri Press.

Holdt, Jacob. 1985. *American pictures: A personal journey through the American underclass*. Copenhagen: American Pictures Foundation.

Illich, Ivan. 1977. *Disabling professions*. London: M. Boyars.

Jackson, Bruce. 1985. Things that from a long way off look like flies. *Journal of American Folklore* 98; no. 388: 131–47.

———. 1977. *Killing time*. Ithaca: Cornell University Press.

Jones, Michael Owen. 1975. *The hand made object and its maker*. Berkeley: University of California Press.

Kidder, Tracy. 1981. *The Soul of a new machine*. Boston: Little, Brown.

Knauth, Percy. 1974. *The metalsmiths*. New York: Time-Life Books.

Korson, George. 1938. *Minstrels of the mine patch*. Philadelphia: University of Pennsylvania Press.

———. 1943. *Coal dust on the fiddle: Songs and stories of the bituminous industry*. Philadelphia: University of Pennsylvania Press.

———. 1960. *Black rock: Mining folklore of the Pennsylvania Dutch*. Baltimore: Johns Hopkins Press.

Koudelka, Josef, and Milan Kundera. 1984. Invasion: Prague 1968. *Aperture*, no. 97: 6–21.

Krebs, Stephanie. 1975. The film elicitation technique. In *Principles of visual anthropology*, ed. Paul Hockings. The Hague: Mouton.

Lancy, David F. 1980. Becoming a blacksmith in Gbarngasu-akwelle. *Anthropology and Education Quarterly* 11, no. 4: 266–74.

Lasansky, Jeanette. 1980. *To draw, upset, and weld: The work of the Pennsylvania rural blacksmith, 1742–1935*. Lewisburg, Pa.: Union County Historical Society, Oral Traditions Project.

Lasch, Christopher. 1979. *The culture of narcissism*. New York: W. W. Norton.

LeMasters, E. E. 1974. *Blue-collar aristocrats: Life-styles at a working-class tavern*. Madison: University of Wisconsin Press.

Lerner, Max, ed. 1948. *The portable Veblen*. New York: Viking.

Levine, Donald N. 1985. *The flight from ambiguity*. Chicago: University of Chicago Press.

Lévi-Strauss, Claude. 1966. *The savage mind*. Chicago: University of Chicago Press; originally published 1962.

Lynd, Robert, and Helen Lynd. 1929. *Middletown: A study in American culture*. New York: Harcourt, Brace and World.

———. 1937. *Middletown in transition*. New York: Harcourt, Brace and World.

Lyon, Danny. 1969. *Conversations with the dead.* New York: Holt, Rinehart and Winston.

MacBean, James. 1983. Beyond observational cinema: The films of David and Judith MacDougall. *Film Quarterly* 36, no. 3.

MacDougall, David. 1974. Beyond observational cinema. In *Principles of visual anthropology,* ed. Paul Hockings. The Hague: Mouton.

Marx, Karl. 1970. *The German ideology.* New York: International Publishers.

Mathers, Michael. 1973. *Riding the rails.* Boston: Gambit.

———. 1975. *Sheepherders: Men alone.* Boston: Houghton Mifflin.

Mead, Margaret, and Gregory Bateson. 1942. *Balinese character.* New York: New York Academy of Sciences.

Messenger, Betty. 1975. *Picking up the linen threads: A study of industrial folklore.* Austin: University of Texas Press.

Needleman, Carla. 1979. *The work of craft.* New York: Alfred A. Knopf.

Nichols, Bill. 1983. The voice of documentary. *Film Quarterly* 36, no. 3: 17–30.

Owens, Bill. 1973. *Suburbia.* San Francisco: Straight Arrow Books.

———. 1975. *Our kind of people: American groups and rituals.* San Francisco: Straight Arrow Books.

Perrow, Charles. 1984. Normal accident at Three Mile Island. In *Critical studies in organization and bureaucracy,* ed. Carmen Sirianni and Frank Fisher. Philadelphia: Temple University Press.

Pirsig, Robert M. 1974. *Zen and the art of motorcycle maintenance: An inquiry into values.* New York: William Morrow.

Riboud, Marc. 1981. *Visions of China.* New York: Random House.

Richards, Dona. 1981. The nyama of the blacksmith: The metaphysical significance of metallurgy in Africa. *Journal of Black Studies* 12, no. 2: 218–38.

Robertson, James. 1981. *American myth, American reality.* New York: Hill and Wang.

Saint Lawrence County Cooperative Extension Association. 1981. *Saint Lawrence agriculture.* Canton, N.Y.: Author.

Saudek, Jan. 1982. Story from Czechoslovakia, my country. *Aperture,* no. 89: 62–76.

Schumacher, E. F. 1973. *Small is beautiful: Economics as if people mattered.* New York: Harper and Row.

Schwartz, Barry. 1973. Waiting, exchange and power: The distribution of time in social systems. *American Journal of Sociology* 79: 841–70.

Shaw, Clifford R. 1970. *The jack-roller: A delinquent boy's own story.* Chicago: University of Chicago Press.

Smith, Cyril Stanley. 1981. *A search for structure.* Cambridge: MIT Press.

Smith, Michael. 1983. *Spirit world.* New Orleans: New Orleans Urban Folklife Society.

Smith, W. Eugene, and Aileen Smith. 1975. *Minamata.* New York: Holt, Rinehart and Winston.

Spradley, James P. 1979. *The ethnographic interview.* Holt, Rinehart and Winston.

Sprague, Stephen. 1978. How I see the Yuroba see themselves. *Studies in the Anthropology of Visual Communication* 5, no. 1: 9–28.

Stadtfeld, Curtis. 1972. *From the land and back.* New York: Scribner's.

Stehle, Bernard. 1985. *Incurably romantic.* Philadelphia: Temple University Press.

Sudnow, David. 1978. *The ways of the hand: The organization of improvised conduct.* Cambridge: Harvard University Press.

———. 1979. *Talk's body: A meditation between two keyboards.* New York: Alfred A. Knopf.

Taylor, Frederick Winslow. 1911. *The principles of scientific management.* New York: Harper and Row.

Tucker, Robert C., ed. 1972. *The Marx-Engels reader.* New York: W. W. Norton.

U.S. Bureau of the Census. 1927. *United States census of agriculture.* Washington, D.C.: U.S. Government Printing Office.

———. 1982. *1980 census of population,* vol. 1, part 3. Washington, D.C.: U.S. Government Printing Office.

Veblen, Thorstein. 1914. *The instinct of workmanship and the state of industrial arts.* New York: Viking.

———, trans. 1925. *The Laxdaela saga.* With an introduction. New York: B. W. Huebsch.

Vidich, Arthur, and Joseph Bensman. 1958. *Small town in mass society.* Princeton: Princeton University Press.

Vidich, Arthur, Joseph Bensman, and Maurice Stein, eds. 1964. *Reflections on community studies.* New York: John Wiley.

Wagner, Jon. 1979. *Images of information.* Beverly Hills, Calif.: Sage.

Weizenbaum, Joseph. 1976. *Computer power and human reason: From judgment to calculation.* San Francisco: W. H. Freeman.

White, Lynn, Jr. 1962. *Medieval technology and social change.* London: Oxford University Press.

Whyte, William Foote. 1984. *Learning from the field: A guide from experience.* Beverly Hills, Calif.: Sage.

Zerubavel, Eviatar. 1981. *Hidden rhythms: Schedules and calendars in social life.* Chicago: University of Chicago Press.

Index